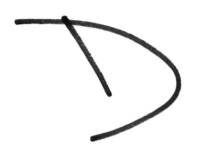

Barack Obama

Black Americans of Achievement

LEGACY EDITION

Martin Luther King, Jr.
Barack Obama
Rosa Parks
Oprah Winfrey
Tiger Woods

Barack Obama

Heather Lehr Wagner

☑®
Checkmark Books™
An imprint of Facts On File, Inc.

Barack Obama

Checkmark Books
An imprint of Infobase Publishing
132 West 31st Street
New York NY 10001

Library of Congress Cataloging-in-Publication Data

Wagner, Heather Lehr.
  Barack Obama / Heather Lehr Wagner.
      p. cm. — (Black Americans of achievement, legacy edition)
  Includes bibliographical references and index.
  ISBN 978-1-60413-324-0 (pbk.)
  1. Obama, Barack. 2. Legislators—United States—Biography. 3. African American legislators—Biography. 4. Presidential candidates—United States—Biography. 5. United States. Congress. Senate—Biography. 6. United States—Politics and government—2001– 7. Illinois—Politics and government—1951– I. Title. II. Series.

  E901.1.O23W25 2008
  328.73092—dc22
  [B]   2007045642

Checkmark books are available at special discounts when purchased in bulk quantities for businesses, associations, institutions, or sales promotions. Please call our Special Sales Department in New York at (212) 967-8800 or (800) 322-8755.

You can find Infobase Publishing on the World Wide Web at
 http://www.infobasepublishing.com

Series design by Keith Trego
Cover design by Keith Trego and Jooyoung An

Printed in the United States of America

Bang ML 10 9 8 7 6 5 4 3 2 1

This book is printed on acid-free paper.

All links and web addresses were checked and verified to be correct at the time of publication. Because of the dynamic nature of the web, some addresses and links may have changed since publication and may no longer be valid.

Contents

1 A Campaign Begins   1

2 Family Origins   7

3 Childhood   16

4 Troubled Youth   27

5 Community Organizer   38

6 Legal Training   50

7 Illinois State Senator   59

8 Campaign for the U.S. Senate   70

9 The Senator From Illinois   80

  Chronology   92

  Further Reading   93

  Index   94

  About the Author and Picture Credits   98

1

A Campaign Begins

On February 10, 2007, a crowd of more than 15,000 people gathered outside the Old State Capitol building in Springfield, Illinois. The Capitol, chosen as the backdrop for this gathering, is rich in historical connections. Although the building is a reconstruction, it was on this site that Abraham Lincoln delivered his famous "House Divided" speech in 1858, boldly stating, "I believe this government cannot endure, permanently half slave and half free." That speech that marked the beginning of his campaign for the U.S. Senate. As an attorney and politician, Lincoln spent a lot of time at the Capitol. As a state legislator, he had been involved in the campaign to relocate the Illinois capital from Vandalia to Springfield in 1837. Lincoln used the building for meetings during his 1860 presidential campaign, and, after his assassination, his body lay in state in its Representatives Hall.

On February 10, 2007, U.S. Senator Barack Obama announced that he was running for president in 2008 in Springfield, Illinois. Above, Obama and his wife, Michelle, wave to the cheering crowd following the announcement.

On that February day, however, the crowd had gathered in the 12°F (−11°C) chill for another historic scene. In that setting, the 45-year-old junior senator from Illinois, Barack Obama, appeared to cheers and applause and said, "In the shadow of the Old State Capitol, where Lincoln once called on a divided house to stand together, where common hopes and common dreams still live, I stand before you today to announce my candidacy for president of the United States."

Obama continued to connect his campaign to the legacy of Lincoln, stating to the crowd, "You came here because you believe in what this country can be. You believe that we can be one people, reaching out for what's possible, building that more perfect union." His announcement included a mention of a key campaign issue: "Let's be the generation that says, right here, right now, we will have universal health care in America by the end of the next president's first term."

The announcement of a presidential campaign was not unexpected, but the enthusiasm with which it was greeted underscored how deeply Obama, in only a few years of public life, had connected with voters. The location was personally significant for Obama, as well. He had begun his political career in Springfield just 10 years earlier, serving for 8 years in the Illinois legislature before his election to the U.S. Senate in 2004.

During his announcement, Obama referred to his relative lack of experience in national politics and turned it into an asset. "I recognize there is a certain presumptuousness, a certain audacity, to this announcement," he said. "I know I haven't spent a lot of time learning the ways of Washington. But I've been there long enough to know that the ways of Washington must change."

IN HIS OWN WORDS...

In the epilogue to his best-selling autobiography, *Dreams From My Father: A Story of Race and Inheritance*, Barack Obama noted that American law offers a kind of long conversation, revealing the ways in which the nation has argued with its conscience:

> What is our community, and how might that community be reconciled with our freedom? How far do our obligations reach? How do we transform mere power into justice, mere sentiment into love? The answers I find in law books don't always satisfy me—for every *Brown v. Board of Education* I find a score of cases where conscience is sacrificed to expedience or greed. And yet, in the conversation itself, in the joining of voices, I find myself modestly encouraged, believing that so long as the questions are still being asked, what binds us together might somehow, ultimately, prevail.

Obama's speech was designed to inspire his supporters with a call to service. "This campaign has to be about reclaiming the meaning of citizenship," he said. "It must be about what we can do together." In the speech, he also drew a line between older politicians—many of them his rivals for the presidency—and what he described as "a new generation," stating that the time had come for this new generation to answer the call to service.

Many of those gathered outside the Old State Capitol knew little about Obama's background or his voting record in the Senate. They had come to hear him speak not necessarily because of his political platform, or his position on key issues, or his vision for the country. They had come because of what Barack Obama represented—a change from the politics that had led the United States into an unpopular war in Iraq, a belief in a better life and a better America, a desire for a different kind of politician. They came because of what Obama called "the audacity of hope."

A TRANSFORMING SPEECH

It was a speech at the Democratic National Convention on July 27, 2004—a speech titled "The Audacity of Hope"—that first propelled Barack Obama into the national spotlight. In a keynote address designed to encourage voters to support Democratic presidential candidate John Kerry, Obama shared the details of his own life story. He told of his father, who grew up herding goats in a small village in Kenya, and eventually traveled to America as a foreign student on a scholarship. He told of his paternal grandfather, who had worked as a domestic servant and a cook, and of his maternal grandfather, who had enlisted in the military after Pearl Harbor and served under General Patton. He told of his mother, who had been born in Kansas and moved west with her family as they searched for greater economic opportunities.

"I stand here today," Obama told the audience, "grateful for the diversity of my heritage, aware that my parents' dreams live

In the midst of his campaign for a seat in the U.S. Senate, Illinois state senator Barack Obama was chosen to give the keynote address at the 2004 Democratic National Convention. Above, Obama addresses the convention on July 27, 2004, in Boston.

on in my precious daughters. I stand here knowing that my story is part of the larger American story, that I owe a debt to all of those who came before me, and that, in no other country on earth, is my story even possible."

In one of the most electrifying moments of his speech, Obama challenged the nation to defy those seeking to divide voters with labels and negative campaign ads: "There's not a liberal America and a conservative America—there's the United States of America. There's not a black America and white America and Latino America and Asian America; there's the United States of America."

Within hours of that keynote address, Barack Obama was being discussed as a possible candidate for president of the

United States. Three months later, he was elected to the U.S. Senate with 70 percent of the vote. Then, just two and a half years later, he stood before a crowd in Springfield, Illinois, and announced the start of his presidential campaign.

Barack Obama was not the first African-American candidate to run for president, but his campaign for the 2008 presidential election was noteworthy for several reasons. He quickly emerged as a frontrunner in a crowded field of highly qualified candidates, despite his relative lack of political experience. This same lack of extensive political experience offered him another advantage—the ability to speak for a "new generation" seeking a change in their leadership.

2

Family Origins

The story of Barack Obama begins in Hawaii. He was born in Honolulu on August 4, 1961, to Kansas-born Ann Dunham and Barack Obama Sr., a student from Kenya. The younger Obama's full name—Barack Hussein Obama Jr.—was inherited from his father. Barack means "blessed by God" in Swahili. This name was one of the few pieces of his father's history that would be clear to Obama for much of his life. In the introduction to his autobiography, *Dreams From My Father*, Obama states, "I learned long ago to distrust my childhood and the stories that shaped it." This suspicion stems from a childhood marked by change and unanswered questions.

Obama was born in a state that had joined the United States only two years earlier. There was a strong U.S. military presence on the Hawaiian island of Oahu, where Obama took his first steps. Although Hawaii reflected the idea of America as a "melting pot," it was still uncommon at that time for a white woman and a black man to date, let alone to marry.

Obama's mother, whose full name was Stanley Ann Dunham (she was named for her father, who had hoped she would be a boy), was not worried about conventions or social customs, however. Eighteen years old and a student at the University of Hawaii when she gave birth to Barack, she was a woman who, according to her son, "saw mysteries everywhere and took joy in the sheer strangeness of life." Her joy would be tested when her husband left her and their two-year-old son to attend graduate school at Harvard University.

Barack Obama Sr. only returned to Hawaii once. By then, his son was 10 years old. They spent one month together before Barack Obama Sr. went back to Kenya. Those few weeks would deeply affect the future politician, though, leaving him wrestling with questions about his identity, his history, and what kind of man he wanted to be. The answers would come many years later, when Barack Obama Jr. would travel to Kenya and begin to piece together the mystery of who his father was and where he had come from.

KENYAN ROOTS

Obama's search for his roots took him to Kenya, in East Africa. Obama knew that his family belonged to the *Luo* tribe, one of the largest groups in Kenya. Shortly before his father's visit, 10-year-old Obama had boasted to his friends that his father was a prince who would take over the tribe when his grandfather died. He told them that his father was a warrior and that the name Obama meant "Burning Spear."

The stories young Barack told, however, were based on little more than his imagination and a few jumbled bits of Kenyan history. "Burning Spear," for example, was actually the nickname of Jomo Kenyatta, the first president of Kenya. Obama finally went to the library and researched the Luo, learning to his disappointment that the reality was far less romantic than

As an adult, Barack Obama traveled to Kenya in order to explore his roots. Above, Obama walks with his paternal grandmother, Sarah Hussein Obama, on a visit to his father's home, Nyangoma village in the Siaya District.

he had imagined—the Luo were a cattle-raising people who lived in mud huts and ate cornmeal and yams.

As an adult, Obama's first impression of Kenya was of a kind of homecoming, a sense of belonging, despite his lack of knowledge about his father and his roots. At the airport, an employee—upon learning his last name—expressed her sympathy about his father's death. "For the first time in my life," Obama wrote in *Dreams of My Father*, "I felt the comfort, the firmness of identity that a name might provide, how it could carry an entire history in other people's memories."

What Obama learned as he traveled through Kenya, spending time with his half-siblings and other relatives, was that his ancestral roots lay in Nyang'oma, a tiny farming village in western Kenya. Both Obama's father and grandfather are buried there, outside a modest tin-roofed home where members of Obama's family still live.

In Kenya, Obama learned that his paternal grandfather, Hussein Onyango, was born in 1895. That year, the British began a massive construction project in Kenya—a railway that would run some 600 miles (966 kilometers), from the city of Mombasa on the Indian Ocean to the eastern shores of Lake Victoria. Obama's step-grandmother told him that his grandfather was among the first to interact with the white men who came to their region of Kenya. He eventually began to wear Western-style clothing, and he learned to read and write English. He worked for the British and was eventually sent to Tanganyika and then to Nairobi. Because Africans were not allowed to travel on the train that crossed their land, Obama's grandfather made these journeys on foot, walking for more than two weeks to reach his assignment in Nairobi and fighting off leopards, snakes, and even an angry buffalo.

Onyango was hired as a domestic servant, preparing food and running the estates of many wealthy British settlers. By saving his earnings, he eventually bought some land and cattle and built a hut. His neighbors found his Westernized customs strange: He insisted that visitors remove their shoes or rinse their feet before entering his hut. He ate all of his meals at a table and chair, with a knife and fork, under mosquito netting. Obama's half-brother and -sister told him that they called their grandfather "the Terror" because he made them sit at the table for dinner, eat their food on china, and beat them with a stick if they said the wrong thing or used the wrong fork. He bathed constantly and washed his clothes every night. In keeping with Muslim custom, Onyango took several wives. His first wife, Akumu, was the mother of Barack Obama Sr.

During World War II, Onyango traveled as a cook for a British captain. He was gone for three years. When he was 50 years old, he decided to stop working for the British and resume farming. He eventually sold his cattle and focused his energy on growing plants and herbs.

Onyango was often abusive to his wives, and Akumu finally ran away, leaving her son and daughter behind. Barack Obama Jr. learned that his father, as a young boy, had tried to find his mother. He and his sister snuck away late one night and spent two weeks on foot, begging for food and sleeping in fields, until a woman took them in, fed them, and then returned them to their father.

Obama's father was remembered by many as mischievous and clever as a boy. His father taught him numbers and letters, and school came easy to him. He seldom attended classes, but he would study the book and then, a few days before the exams, he would take the tests and usually be first in his class.

QUEST FOR INDEPENDENCE

By the time Barack Obama Sr. was a teenager, an independence movement was growing in Kenya. The teenager was intrigued by the discussions. His father, having seen the power and vastness of the British military, was skeptical that a revolt against the British could succeed. Despite his attitude, Onyango was placed in a detention camp for six months, falsely accused of being a supporter of the revolutionary movement. When he finally returned home, he was feeble and sick and never fully recovered.

At the time of his father's detention, Barack Obama Sr. was at a secondary school 50 miles (80 kilometers) away. He had been selected for admission to the elite mission school, but he quickly got into trouble for sneaking girls into the dormitory and stealing food from nearby farms, and he was eventually expelled.

Onyango was furious when he learned of his son's expulsion. He forced his son to take a job in Mombasa, on the Kenyan coast, explaining that he would only appreciate the value of an education when he had to earn his own living. Barack Obama Sr. worked there only briefly, eventually securing a job as a railway clerk in Nairobi. There, Obama began to attend political meetings. At 18 he married his first wife, Kezia, and they soon had a son and daughter. After being arrested for his involvement in the revolutionary movement, he was determined to focus on earning a living. He began to notice that his friends were leaving Kenya for further study in Uganda or London, and that when they returned they had good jobs waiting for them.

Obama befriended two American women teaching in Nairobi who loaned him books and encouraged him to focus on his education. With their support, he applied to several American universities for scholarships. The University of Hawaii responded positively. Barack Obama Sr. did not know anything about Hawaii when he left his family and traveled to Honolulu.

It was 1959, and Barack Obama Sr. was 23 years old. He would become the University of Hawaii's first African student and would study economics. He helped organize the International Students Association, becoming its first president. He would eventually graduate in three years with top honors. It was in a Russian language course at the university that he would meet Ann Dunham.

A GIRL FROM KANSAS

Stanley Ann Dunham, known as Ann, lived with her parents in Honolulu. The family had moved to Hawaii from Kansas in 1959, arriving the same year as Barack Obama Sr.

When Barack Obama Jr. announced his candidacy for the presidency, the *New York Times* reported that genealogists who traced his family origins would discover that his mother's ancestors had been slave owners. The genealogists learned that Obama's great-great-great-great-grandfather, George Washington Overall, had owned two slaves, according to 1850 census records for Nelson County, Kentucky. His great-great-great-great-great-grandmother, Mary Duval, also owned two slaves. Records showed that Obama was distantly related to Jefferson Davis, the president of the Confederacy, whereas another ancestor had fought for the Union in the Civil War.

Obama spent much of his childhood living with his maternal grandparents, Stanley and Madelyn Dunham. It is interesting to note that Stanley Dunham had also spent much of his childhood with his grandparents, who had raised him after his father disappeared and his mother committed suicide. Both of Obama's maternal grandparents grew up in small towns in Kansas, Stanley in El Dorado and Madelyn in Augusta. It was the time of the Great Depression. Madelyn's father worked for an oil refinery and her mother was a schoolteacher.

Stanley had discovered his mother's body after her suicide. He was eight years old. When he was 15, he was expelled from high school for punching the principal. He spent the next three years working odd jobs and traveling by train to Chicago and California. Eventually he ended up in Wichita, Kansas, where his grandparents had relocated. It was there that he met Madelyn, whose family had also moved to Wichita.

Madelyn's parents had learned of Stanley's reputation and did their best to discourage their daughter from dating him. Their efforts failed. The couple eloped shortly before the bombing of Pearl Harbor, and when the war began, Stanley enlisted in the armed services. Obama's mother was born at an army base where her own mother worked as a riveter while her father served in France under General Patton.

When the war ended, Stanley Dunham moved the family to California. The GI Bill funded his education at the University of California at Berkeley, but he did not stay there long, first moving the family back to Kansas, then to Texas, and finally to Seattle, where Obama's mother completed high school.

According to Obama's autobiography, it was in Texas that the family encountered strong racism. As a furniture salesman, Stanley Dunham was told by his coworkers that black and Hispanic customers could only come to the store after hours and then needed to make their own arrangements for delivering the furniture they might buy. Madelyn Dunham, working at a bank, was told by a colleague not to address the black janitor as "Mister."

Obama also noted that, at age 11, his mother befriended a black girl but was harassed by the other children, who followed them to the Dunham house and threw stones at them until her mother arrived to chase them away. Stanley complained to the principal and to the parents of the other children, who all told him that his daughter needed to learn not to play with children who were not white.

Later, Stanley Dunham told his grandson that these incidents were the main reason the family left Texas. Obama's grandmother disputed this memory, though. She said that the family left for Seattle because Stanley had been promised a better job. In Seattle, Obama's mother applied to several colleges. She was offered admission to the University of Chicago but her father refused to allow her to go, saying that she was too young to live on her own. Instead, the family moved to

IN HIS OWN WORDS...

In *The Audacity of Hope*, Barack Obama wrote of his mother's kindness, her outrage at poverty and injustice, and her sense of wonder for life and nature:

It is only in retrospect, of course, that I fully understand how deeply this spirit of hers influenced me—how it sustained me despite the absence of a father in the house, how it buoyed me through the rocky shoals of my adolescence, and how it invisibly guided the path I would ultimately take. My fierce ambitions might have been fueled by my father—by my knowledge of his achievements and failures, by my unspoken desire to somehow earn his love, and by my resentments and anger toward him. But it was my mother's fundamental faith—in the goodness of people and in the ultimate value of this brief life we've each been given—that channeled those ambitions.

Hawaii, where Ann Dunham enrolled in the university and soon met a dynamic fellow student named Barack Obama.

A YOUNG FAMILY

Obama would note later that details about his parent's engagement and marriage were seldom shared, and that he knew little about the brief time they spent together. "There's no record of a real wedding," he wrote in *Dreams From My Father*. "Just a small civil ceremony, a justice of the peace. The whole thing seems so fragile in retrospect, so haphazard. And perhaps that's how my grandparents intended it to be, a trial that would pass, just a matter of time, so long as they maintained a stiff upper lip and didn't do anything drastic."

Barack Obama Sr. did write to his family in Kenya to tell them of his new wife. His father wrote back expressing his concern, noting his doubts that a young white American would be willing to move back to Kenya to share her husband with his other wife and children.

Obama's mother later told him that she had planned to move back to Kenya with her husband, despite her parents' objection and fears for her safety. When Barack Obama Sr. graduated from the University of Hawaii, however, he received two scholarships. One was a full scholarship to the New School in New York City. The scholarship paid for room and board, a job on campus, and enough to support the student and his family. The other scholarship was to Harvard University. That scholarship only covered tuition.

Barack Obama Sr. chose the scholarship to Harvard. "How can I refuse the best education?" he asked his wife, despite the fact that it would mean leaving her and his son behind. After completing his studies in Boston, Barack Obama Sr. went back to Kenya. He returned to Hawaii only once. By then, his son was 10 years old.

3

Childhood

Barack Obama spent his earliest years living with his mother and grandparents in Honolulu. Ann Dunham ultimately divorced Barack's father and soon met another foreign student studying at the University of Hawaii. Lolo Soetoro was from Indonesia—his name meant "crazy" in Hawaiian, a source of great amusement to Barack and his grandfather.

In *Dreams From My Father*, Barack Obama would describe Soetoro as patient and polite: "He was short and brown, handsome, with thick black hair and features that could have as easily been Mexican or Samoan as Indonesian; his tennis game was good, his smile uncommonly even, and his temperament imperturbable." Obama's mother first brought Lolo Soetoro home to meet her son and parents when Barack was four, and for the next two years Soetoro would patiently play chess with Ann's father and wrestle with her son. Finally, when Barack was six years old, his mother and Lolo Soetoro became engaged.

Soetoro quickly left Hawaii—what Barack did not know until much later was that his visa had been revoked and he was being called back to Indonesia for military service. Ann made the preparations for her and her son to join him. As Ann busied herself with arranging the paperwork—plane tickets, passports, visas—Barack's grandfather would show him where Indonesia was on an atlas and speculate about whether or not Barack might see tigers, orangutans, and even headhunters. Barack's grandmother phoned the State Department to determine whether or not Indonesia was stable. It was 1967, and only two years earlier a military coup had resulted in violence and the massacre of thousands. Reassured by the government's

General Suharto

Two years before Barack Obama arrived in Indonesia, the country experienced a dramatic shift in power. The military, led by the little-known General Suharto, seized power over a country that Suharto would rule for more than 30 years. Claiming that the country was under threat from Communist influences, Suharto launched a brutal program to suppress any traces of Communism, and hundreds of thousands of suspected Communist sympathizers were killed.

In March 1967, Suharto was installed as president. Suharto claimed to be a farmer's son who had participated in his country's independence movement against the Dutch. Under Suharto's leadership, Indonesia became an oil-producing nation, and the oil revenue helped fund large-scale development. Suharto also sought to develop greater ties with Western nations and was able to bring significant Western investment to Indonesia. Obama's stepfather reflected this transition, serving first in the military and later working for an oil company.

Despite periods of economic growth, Indonesia suffered under Suharto. His regime brutally crushed any who opposed it, and there was widespread corruption, with only a select group benefiting from the country's economic growth.

On May 21, 1988, General Suharto was finally forced to resign when key members of his staff deserted him and the streets of Jakarta filled with student protestors.

response, his grandmother then began to pack large trunks full of food, including powdered drink mix, powdered milk, cans of sardines, and even boxes of candy.

It took three days for the family to travel to Indonesia, with a stopover in Japan, where Barack later remembered eating green tea ice cream on a ferry while his mother studied flash cards to help her learn her new husband's language. Then they were in Indonesia, and six-year-old Barack suddenly found himself immersed in a new life with a new stepfather surrounded by people speaking a language he did not understand.

The family settled in Jakarta, in a neighborhood more like a village than the urban setting Barack had known in Honolulu. Villagers still bathed and washed their clothes in the river. There were more cycle rickshaws than cars in the streets.

His stepfather's home was one of the nicer in the neighborhood—it was made of stucco and red tile, whereas many of the homes nearby were bamboo huts. Electricity had only recently arrived in the neighborhood. The house did not have air-conditioning, refrigeration, or flush toilets.

A large mango tree stood in front of Barack's new home. When he first arrived at the house, Barack was startled when a large ape jumped out of the tree—his stepfather had bought him as a pet for Barack. Chickens, ducks, dogs, birds of paradise, and cockatoos roamed the backyard, and baby crocodiles swam in a fenced-off pond near the back of the house.

DIFFERENT STORIES

In *Dreams From My Father*, Obama described a relatively idyllic childhood in Indonesia:

> It had taken me less than six months to learn Indonesia's language, its customs and its legends. I had survived chicken pox, measles, and the sting of my teachers' bamboo switches. The children of farmers, servants, and low-level bureaucrats

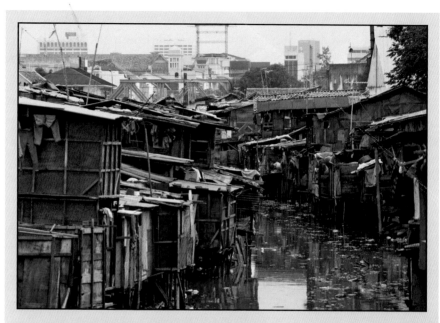

The photo above from 1995 shows what housing is like for the poorest residents of Jakarta, Indonesia. When Obama moved with his mother to Jakarta, their home was surrounded by areas like this.

had become my best friends, and together we ran the streets morning and night, hustling odd jobs, catching crickets, battling swift kites with razor-sharp lines.

He described his stepfather teaching him to box. He told of learning to eat new foods, such as raw green chili peppers, dog meat, snake meat, and roasted grasshopper.

Chicago Tribune journalists Kirsten Scharnberg and Kim Barker, who interviewed those who remember Obama from Indonesia, reported a different, and far more difficult experience for the future presidential candidate, however. In Indonesia, Obama was known as "Barry Soetoro" and was a chubby boy teased by the children in the neighborhood because of his physical appearance. He was the only foreign child in the neighborhood and the only one to attend the new Catholic school nearby. Most families in the neighborhood were Betawis, Jakarta natives who were traditional Muslims.

One man who had been one of Obama's neighbors when both were boys remembered that, when Obama followed them one day, he and some others threw Obama into the swamp. Teachers remembered him as quiet, struggling to learn the language, and, as a result, finding school difficult. His first-grade teacher recalled trying to help him master Indonesian by going over pronunciation and vowel sounds, feeling sorry for the shy boy who always sat in the back of the classroom. His elementary school teachers also recognized many of the traits that would emerge in the adult—a sense of compassion for those younger and less fortunate, a desire to help others. In third grade, Obama wrote an essay on what he wanted to be when he grew up. In the essay, Obama said that he wanted to be president—he did not mention which country he wanted to be president of, but he did say that he wanted to make every-body happy.

Obama noted that certain horrifying events did shape his life in Jakarta. He was often frightened of the deformed beg-gars who knocked on the door of the family home, asking for food. For the first time, he understood the impact of drought and heavy rains on the farms nearby. His friends spoke matter-of-factly of exorcisms or the death of siblings.

Money was tight for the family. Obama's stepfather was working for the Indonesian army as a geologist, surveying roads and tunnels. The work did not pay very much, and Obama's mother soon found a job as an English teacher at the American embassy. Eventually, Obama's stepfather got a better job, working in the government relations office of an Ameri-can oil company. The family's finances improved. Obama's stepfather bought a car to replace the motorcycle that had been the family's only transportation. When Obama was in fourth grade, they were able to move to a better neighborhood. The new community traditionally housed foreign business owners and diplomats and was marked by gated homes, wide roads, and lush green plants. Here the family had a television and a stereo.

Obama was enrolled in a new school, this time a Muslim one. In the same way that young Barack was expected to adapt to a new language, a new culture, and the Catholic teachings of his previous school, he was now expected to adapt to the Muslim school with its different religious traditions.

Just as he had at his old school, Obama sat in the back of the classroom. One friend remembered him spending much of his time drawing American superheroes, such as Spider-Man and Batman. He attended the school for about a year before suddenly disappearing. The few friends he had made were told simply that he had moved.

RETURN TO AMERICA

The marriage between Obama's mother and stepfather had been troubled for several years. The birth of Obama's half-sister, Maya, brought a brief time of happiness for the couple, but Obama writes in his autobiography of hearing them arguing, usually over his mother's refusal to attend her husband's business parties.

Obama was even more aware of a difference in his mother's attitude toward him. When they first arrived in Jakarta, she had encouraged him to learn the language, adapt to Indonesian culture, and spend time with his stepfather. As her marriage deteriorated, though, she enrolled her son in an American correspondence course to supplement his studies. She woke him at 4:00 A.M., gave him a quick breakfast, and then spent three hours teaching him in English before she left for work and Obama left for school.

As an adult, Obama understood that his mother's concerns extended to fears about his health and worries about the differences between her own personal values and the values of the society in which they lived. In one incident, Obama was injured on a barbed wire fence and returned home after dark with a large gash on his arm. Obama's stepfather refused to take the boy to the hospital until the following morning, so his mother instead begged a neighbor with a car to drive them to the hospital.

The hospital was in near darkness when they arrived, and Obama's mother had to search through the hallways until finally locating two doctors, who wore only boxer shorts as they played checkers. Obama still bears a scar on his arm from the 20 stitches the doctors finally gave him that night.

Ann began to talk increasingly about Obama's father, praising his intelligence, his honesty, and his willingness to work hard. She encouraged Obama to be proud of his heritage and often spoke admiringly of Rosa Parks, Martin

DID YOU KNOW?

Barack Obama often speaks of his unique heritage—his mother came from Kansas, his father from Kenya—and his experiences as a child in Hawaii and as an adult in Chicago. Obama lived for four years—from the age of 6 until he was 10—in Indonesia, though, and its culture also contributed to his heritage and to his view of America's role in the world.

In *The Audacity of Hope,* Barack Obama wrote of the Indonesia he had known as a boy and his conflicting desire to take his wife and daughters there:

> When I think of . . . Indonesia, I'm haunted by memories—the feel of packed mud under bare feet as I wander through paddy fields; the sight of day breaking behind volcanic peaks; the muezzin's call at night and the smell of wood smoke; the dickering at the fruit stands alongside the road. . . . I would like to take Michelle and the girls to share that piece of my life, to climb the thousand-year-old Hindu ruins of Prambanan or swim in a river high in Balinese hills. But my plans for such a trip keep getting delayed. I'm chronically busy, and traveling with young children is always difficult. And, too, perhaps I am worried about what I will find there—that the land of my childhood will no longer match my memories.

Luther King Jr., and other heroes of the civil rights struggle in the United States.

In 1971, 10-year-old Barack Obama was sent back to Hawaii. His mother had enrolled him at Punahou Academy, an elite private school in Oahu. Obama began fifth grade there and attended the school until his graduation in 1979, one of the few black pupils at a school with students who were mostly white and Asian, and from Hawaii's wealthiest families.

PUNAHOU SCHOOL

Obama's grandparents helped arrange his admission to the prestigious Punahou School. His grandfather's boss, an alumnus of the school, helped get Barack onto the admissions list.

Obama's grandfather accompanied Barack to school on his first day. His new teacher quickly explained that she had lived in Kenya. Obama writes of being embarrassed when she suggested that he use his given name of Barack ("such a beautiful name") rather than Barry and then asked which tribe his family belonged to.

Obama writes of feeling that he did not belong in his new life:

> The clothes that Gramps and I had chosen for me were too old-fashioned; the Indonesian sandals that had served me so well in Djakarta were dowdy. Most of my classmates had been together since kindergarten; they lived in the same neighborhoods, in split-level homes with swimming pools; their fathers coached the same Little League teams; their mothers sponsored the bake sales. Nobody played soccer or badminton or chess, and I had no idea how to throw a football in a spiral or balance on a skateboard.

In an editorial in the *New York Times*, Lawrence Downes writes of understanding Obama's sense of alienation in Hawaii. Downes himself had been a student in Hawaii in

While a senior at Punahou, Obama participated in the Ka Wai Ola ("the waters of life") Club, a literary magazine featuring poetry and prose written by Punahou's high school students. He is pictured above with other members.

the 1970s, noting that Punahou had a reputation as an elite school. "For Mr. Obama, fitting in at Punahou could have been hard, given its reputation as a cliquish school dominated since missionary days by the rich white people who founded it. Mr. Obama, a scholarship student, wasn't rich and didn't look white."

Life with his grandparents added to Obama's sense of alienation. His grandparents had sold the large home near the university in which Obama had lived as a young boy and moved into a small, two-bedroom apartment in a high-rise building. They no longer took Obama on hikes or to the beach. They stayed in the tiny apartment and watched television or read.

Obama's grandfather was struggling to earn a living as a life insurance salesman. His grandmother was more successful, rising early each morning to catch the 6:30 A.M. bus downtown, where she worked as a bank executive.

Obama walked to and from school each day. His grandfather was waiting when he got home. Later in the afternoon, the two would drive downtown to pick up his grandmother from work. The family ate dinner every night in front of the television.

One student who was at Punahou at the same time as Obama told Scharnberg and Barker, "Punahou was an amazing school. But it could be a lonely place. . . . Those of us who were black did feel isolated—there's no question about that."

A FATHER'S VISIT

After several months, Obama's grandparents received a telegram. His mother would be traveling to Hawaii for Christmas, and his father was also coming to see him.

Obama had no memory of his father. His impressions were based on family stories and the little his mother had told him. When she finally arrived for the holidays, she told Obama that she had written to his father and told him all about their son. She told him that his father had remarried and that he now had five brothers and a sister in Kenya. His father had been in a car accident; he had been hospitalized and would be recovering in Hawaii. With the little information he had, Obama began making up stories about his father and sharing them with his classmates.

Obama's teacher let him leave school early the day his father arrived. When he reached his grandparents' apartment, his first impression was of a tall, thin, dark man who walked with a limp and used a cane.

"Well, Barry," his father said. "It's a good thing to see you after so long. Very good." His father stayed for only a month. During that time they listened to African music, and his father tried to teach him how to dance. They celebrated Christmas with gifts and a photograph—the only picture Obama would ever have of him and his father together. They attended a jazz concert and spent time together reading. His father came to Obama's school and spoke to his class, impressing the students with his stories of wild animals and tribal customs, and of Kenya's struggle for independence.

Then he was gone. That single month would be the last time Obama saw his father and would provide the basis for all his memories of this parent. It was a brief time, and over the next few years, Obama would struggle with his identity, trying to make sense of all the cultures that had formed him. There was Kenya, Kansas, Indonesia, and Hawaii. Later he attended college in California, New York, and Massachusetts. As a young man, though, Obama began to identify himself as African American, an African American from Chicago, the city where he would launch his political career.

4

Troubled Youth

Not long after Obama settled into the routine of life with his grandparents, that routine was disrupted. His mother and stepfather separated, and his mother returned to Hawaii with her baby daughter. She began taking classes to pursue a master's degree in anthropology and rented a small apartment a block away from Obama's school.

For three years, the family lived on the modest financial support his mother's student grants provided. Obama remembered being acutely aware of how different his life was from that of his classmates. He wrote in *Dreams From My Father*,

> Sometimes, when I brought friends home after school, my mother would overhear them remark about the lack of food in the fridge or the less-than-perfect housekeeping, and she would pull me aside and let me know that she was a single mother going to school again and raising two kids, so that

baking cookies wasn't exactly at the top of her priority list, and while she appreciated the fine education I was receiving at Punahou, she wasn't planning on putting up with any snotty attitudes from me or anyone else.

After three years, Obama's mother decided to return to Indonesia to complete her fieldwork. She wanted to enroll Barack and his young half-sister, Maya, at the international school there, but Barack refused to go. He had settled into life at Punahou and did not want to be a new student again. Stanley and Madelyn Dunham, Barack's grandparents, once more agreed to have him live with them. Obama spent a good deal of time with his grandfather and his grandfather's friends.

Some family members and friends saw a hint of Obama's future promise, even in these early years. In Jennifer Steinhauer's article for the *New York Times*, Obama's half-sister Maya recalled, "There was always a joke between my mom and Barack that he would be the first black president. So there were intimations of all this early on. He has always been restless. There was always somewhere else he needed to go."

His homeroom teacher, Eric Kusonoki, remembered Obama's confident walk and cheerful smile. "He had the same exact mannerisms then as he does now," he said. "When he walked up to give that speech at the Democratic convention, we recognized him right away by the way he walked. He was well liked by everybody, a very charismatic guy."

Obama writes of his time at Punahou School as a period of alienation, of wrestling with his identity. As Scharnberg and Barker reported, however, one of his white classmates and close friends later noted that Obama never discussed race or feeling out of place with him: "He was a very provocative thinker. He would bring up worldly topics far beyond his years. But we never talked about race."

In high school, Obama began playing basketball, a sport that showcased his athletic talent and his burgeoning skills at organizing. Above, Obama, a forward and the team's sole left-hander, shoots during a game against a rival team.

FINDING A COMMUNITY

Inspired by his father's Christmas gift—a basketball—and by the success of the University of Hawaii basketball team,

Obama began to play basketball on a playground near his grandparents' apartment. He was awkward at first but gradually his confidence increased. By the time he entered high school, Obama was playing on Punahou's varsity basketball team, although not as a starter, and he finally began to find a circle of friends.

"He was on a very, very strong team," his basketball coach recalled. "Had he been on any other team in the league, he would have been a starter. But he practiced hard, and his work ethic might have been above everyone else's. He practiced at the 10 A.M. juice break; he practiced at the lunch break at noon; and he was the last one to leave each day."

Obama had mastered a long jump shot that earned him the nickname "Barry O'Bomber" from his teammates. The team was so good that they won the state championship in 1979, Obama's senior year.

One teammate remembered that Obama was outspoken in urging the coach to use him and the other second-string players, and to give them equal playing time: "He'd go right up

DID YOU KNOW?

Barack Obama's father gave him a gift on the last Christmas they spent together—a small basketball, a gift inspired in part by the success of the University of Hawaii's basketball team that year. Obama began practicing and soon discovered that the sport provided him with a new community and an outlet for his energy.

Obama played for his high school's varsity team—the team won the state championship during Obama's senior year—and he earned the nickname "Barry O'Bomber" from his teammates for his long jump shot. Obama continued to play in pick-up games throughout college and during his years at Harvard Law School. Every year at Christmas, when Obama returned to Hawaii to visit family, he and some of his friends from high school would once more meet up on the basketball court.

to the coach during a game and say, 'Coach, we're killing this team. Our second string should be playing more.'"

In his autobiography, Obama wrote of finally finding a place where he felt he belonged:

> On the basketball court I could find a community of sorts, with an inner life all its own. It was there that I would make my closest white friends, on turf where blackness couldn't be a disadvantage. And it was there that I could meet Ray and the other blacks close to my age who had begun to trickle into the islands, teenagers whose confusion and anger would help shape my own.

In *Dreams From My Father*, Obama wrote extensively of his friendship with a young man he called "Ray," a student two years older than Obama who had moved to Honolulu from Los Angeles when his father was transferred with the army. "We'd fallen into an easy friendship, due in no small part to the fact that together we made up almost half of Punahou's black high school population." Obama writes of going with Ray to black parties at the University of Hawaii or on the army bases, discussing the perceived racism around them, dividing the world into black and white.

Keith Kakugawa is the actual person on whom the "Ray" character in Obama's book is based. In recent years, he has disputed some of what Obama suggests in his book. To begin with, Kakugawa notes, he is not black; he is biracial like Obama—in his case, half black and half Japanese. He said that at that time they talked less about race than about loneliness. "Barry's biggest struggles then were missing his parents. His biggest struggles were his feelings of abandonment."

There was a group of black students at Punahou who did spend time together informally. They talked about civil rights and racial issues, and they attended parties at the U.S. military

Above is Obama's senior portrait from the 1979 "Oahuan," Punahou's yearbook. Though he seemed to be turning down the wrong path during high school, Obama was accepted to several colleges and began to turn his life around.

bases, with other African Americans. Two members of that group have indicated that Obama did not join them in their activities, however—he spent time with a more racially diverse group of friends.

In the introduction to *Dreams From My Father*, Obama notes that an autobiography presents a special temptation for the author to depict events in the most favorable light and what he calls "selective lapses of memory." The book was written when Obama was 33, working as a lawyer in Chicago and keenly aware of how racism and inequality had shaped that city. His memories of his youth might have been colored by his experiences as an adult.

According to Scharnberg and Barker, Obama's half-sister has noted, however, that Obama

> struggled here with the idea that people were pushing an identity on him [of] what it meant to be a black man. He was trying to balance that with a desire he already had then to name himself. There were not a lot of people here who were engaged in that process. Their identities were more solidly assumed. Having a community that embraced you without question was something that most people had. But he had lived in Indonesia, had a father who was absent but whose presence loomed large and a mother who had lived in 13 places.

What is certain is that Obama became increasingly interested in reading books by black writers, trying to understand what it meant to be a black man. He read about James Baldwin and W.E.B. Du Bois. He read Malcolm X's autobiography. He struggled with how to reconcile the different parts of his identity. He tried to understand how defining himself as African American would affect his relationships with his mother and grandparents.

CHOICES AND CONFLICT

In *Dreams From My Father*, Obama writes frankly that, while in high school, he began drinking alcohol, smoking marijuana, and even using cocaine occasionally:

> Junkie. Pothead. That's where I'd been headed: the final, fatal role of the young would-be black man. Except the highs hadn't been about that, me trying to prove what a

down brother I was. Not by then, anyway. I got high for just
the opposite effect, something that could push questions of
who I was out of my mind, something that could flatten out
the landscape of my heart, blur the edges of my memory.

Obama's candor about his illegal drug use is unusual for a
political candidate, although his memoir was written many years
before he ran for office. He is fortunate to have been able to build
a better life for himself. The friend he identified as "Ray," Keith
Kakugawa, is today a convicted drug felon, who has spent more
than seven years in California prisons and several months in Los
Angeles County Jail on cocaine and auto theft charges.

During this period, Obama's mother was concerned by
the changes in her son, including his poor grades and lack of
ambition. She wrote to him from Indonesia about her life and
work with nonprofit groups doing economic development and
sent advice about the future. She encouraged him to apply to
college, and she and his nine-year-old sister flew to Hawaii in
the spring of 1979 for his high-school graduation.

COLLEGE YEARS

Obama was accepted at several colleges; he chose Occidental
College in Los Angeles. The decision was motivated in part by
a girl from Los Angeles he met while she was on vacation with
her family in Hawaii.

Obama spent two years at Occidental. The college, located
in the small Eagle Rock community, was a tranquil place with
Spanish-tiled buildings and lush green trees. A group of African-American students on campus spent time together. Obama
describes them as a kind of "tribe," who were known for "staying
close together, traveling in packs." Obama lived in a college dorm
his freshman year, then moved into an off-campus apartment.

Although he spent only two years at Occidental, it was during those two years that several significant developments took
place in Obama's life. He began to use the name "Barack" rather

than "Barry," at least among his friends. He encountered a fellow student who encouraged him to focus more on getting his life together than worrying about racial stereotypes and some idealized image of what it meant to be African American. At that time, he also began to take an interest in campus politics.

The issue that first inspired Obama was a divestment campaign—an effort to encourage the college to discontinue support of the government of South Africa (at the time ruled by a white minority who practiced racial discrimination and segregation) by removing its investments in the country. He spoke about the issue at a rally and discovered that he had a gift for inspiring people with his words.

Some of Obama's writing was published in the student magazine *Feast*, including the poem "Pop," a portrait of his grandfather. The poem reveals how, at 19, Obama was making peace with the various parts of his identity, while featuring verses that showed a careful consideration of this man he loved:

Sitting in his seat, a seat broad and broken
In, sprinkled with ashes,
Pop switches channels, takes another
Shot of Seagrams, neat, and asks
What to do with me, a green young man. . . .

Much of Obama's time at Occidental was spent partying, however, and studying was not a priority. Several of his friends graduated or left school, and Obama slowly realized that, if he was to make something of his life, he needed a fresh start in a new place. Occidental had a transfer program with Columbia University in New York City, and Obama decided to leave California and head east.

LIFE IN NEW YORK
Once in New York and enrolled at Columbia, Obama was determined to make a break with the past, particularly with

the bad habits that had marked his time at Occidental College. He found a room in a small apartment with a slanted floor and irregular heat on 94th Street between First and Second Avenues, on the edge of East Harlem. He spent long days walking the streets of New York as a way to keep busy in between classes and as a break from studying. He worked on construction sites during the summer to make money for school. Only family and a few old friends called him "Barry." In New York, he consistently introduced himself as "Barack."

Classmates and teachers at Columbia remember Obama as a serious student, someone who spent a lot of time in the library. In Maurice Possley's article in the March 29, 2007, *Chicago Tribune,* Obama's international politics professor, Michael Baron, recalled that he actively participated in class discussions and wrote a paper on the politics of Soviet–U.S. disarmament talks. The paper earned him an "A." A student in that class noted Obama's maturity: "He was our age, but seemed older because of his poise and the calmness with which he conducted himself. He was a standout in the seminar. He had a kind of a breadth of perspective that a lot of us didn't have."

While he was in New York, only a few months after his twenty-first birthday, Obama received a phone call one morning while making breakfast. The caller identified herself as his Aunt Jane from Nairobi, and she was calling to inform Obama that his father had been killed in a car accident.

Obama phoned his mother, who cried when she heard the news. He did not attend the funeral but instead wrote a letter expressing his sadness to his father's family in Nairobi. He asked them to write to him when they could.

Obama writes in *Dreams From My Father* that he did not truly grieve this loss until nearly a year later when, one night, he dreamed of meeting his father and his father telling him that he loved him:

> I awoke still weeping, my first real tears for him—and for
> me, his jailor, his judge, his son. I turned on the light and

dug out his old letters. I remembered his only visit—the basketball he had given me and how he had taught me to dance. And I realized, perhaps for the first time, how even in his absence his strong image had given me some bulwark on which to grow up, an image to live up to, or disappoint.

Obama focused even more intensely on his studies. Majoring in political science, he periodically participated in activities organized by the Black Students Organization, including antiapartheid protests. Shortly before graduating in 1983, he decided that he would make a career in community organizing. He believed that "communities had to be created, fought for, tended like gardens," and felt that his future was to be found in this kind of work. He began to contact civil rights organizations, black elected officials, neighborhood councils, and tenants' rights groups. No one responded.

Motivated by the very practical need to pay off his student loans, Obama decided to work for whatever company would hire him to make some money and then try again. He was hired as a research assistant for a consulting firm, the only black man in the company, and after a few months was promoted to financial writer with his own office and secretary. He met with Japanese financiers and German bond traders and began to consider the possibility of a career in finance.

That all changed when his half-sister from Kenya, Auma, called. She had planned to come for a visit but had to change her plans because their brother David had been killed in a motorcycle accident. Soon after her call, Obama decided to pursue his dream of finding work as a community organizer. He worked briefly for an environmental organization, then for an unsuccessful candidate running for an assemblyman's position in Brooklyn. Finally, he received a job offer that would change his life: an offer of $10,000 a year to work as a community organizer in a city Obama knew little about: Chicago.

5

Community Organizer

In his book *The Audacity of Hope*, Barack Obama states that his work as an organizer in Chicago "helped me grow into my manhood . . . my work with the pastors and laypeople there deepened my resolve to lead a public life, . . . fortified my racial identity and confirmed my belief in the capacity of ordinary people to do extraordinary things."

Obama had been to Chicago only once before. As a 10-year-old, he took a trip with his grandmother, mother, and sister Maya to see the United States. They traveled to Seattle, went along the coast of California to Disneyland, headed east to the Grand Canyon, and visited Kansas City, the Great Lakes, and Yellowstone Park. They traveled on Greyhound buses and stayed in modest motels, spending three days in Chicago in a motel with an indoor swimming pool. This pool was very impressive to the young Obama, since he had never seen an indoor pool in Hawaii.

Obama returned to Chicago to work 14 years later. He spent his first few days exploring the city before beginning his job. He was hired by a small organization in a part of south Chicago that had been impacted by the closing of the Wisconsin Steel plant, the area's biggest employer. He would be working with two church-based organizations that had been created to help support the impoverished neighborhoods and put pressure on the legislature to help create job placement programs and bring new employment to the region.

The 24-year-old Obama began his work with the Developing Communities Project (DCP), whose mission was to focus on the black neighborhoods that had been affected by the steel plant closing. He was given $2,000 to purchase a rather battered blue Honda Civic, the car he would use for the next three years, driving from one congregation to the next in his effort to organize the neighborhoods. The idea behind community organizing was to create a cohesive neighborhood, to unite those suffering from unemployment over certain key issues so that they could speak with a unified voice and lobby political leaders with their demands—for better schools for their children, for the creation of more jobs, for the training they would need to find new work.

At that time, Chicago had a reputation as being a highly segregated city, but the election of an African-American man, Harold Washington, as mayor had given new hope to the city's black neighborhoods that change might be possible. Obama began by talking to people in the neighborhoods that he was supposed to organize. His goal was to find out what issues people were interested in, and then use that interest to motivate them to get involved. It was difficult work. Many people were reluctant to meet with him. Many were only willing to meet with him in the evening.

Gradually, however, Obama began to gather information about the people with whom he wanted to work. Many had grown up in other parts of Chicago, in more cramped ghettos in the north and west of the city. They had moved south not only for work but because the housing was affordable, there was a bit more space, the schools were better, and the stores were less expensive.

The closing of the steel plant had brought an end to many of their dreams. Suddenly, the future seemed less certain. Their children, once grown, were moving away, and those still in school were dealing with overcrowded classrooms in school and few opportunities if they did graduate. Shops were going out of business. Cars thefts had increased. Parks were empty and unsafe. Children were told to stay indoors. Homes were no longer well maintained, and many houses were boarded up. There was a rise in gang activity.

The challenge for Obama was to find a way to translate what he was hearing into action. The first gatherings he held were poorly attended. He began to try to focus on more specific issues—on things that were concrete and seemed winnable in order to inspire those in the community to get involved.

ALTGELD GARDENS

The Altgeld Gardens public housing project marked Obama's first significant victory. Altgeld Gardens featured about 2,000 apartments in a series of two-story brick buildings with gray-green doors and dirty mock shutters. The apartments were surrounded by waste sites, including the largest landfill in the Midwest and a sewage treatment plant. Fish in the nearby river were discolored and disfigured, and trees planted near the sewage treatment facility did not grow. A heavy odor hung in the air near the housing project, making its way into the apartments even when their doors and windows were shut. There were muddy tire tracks all over the small patches of brown lawn around the buildings.

The insides of the apartments were not much better. Crumbling ceilings marked the places where pipes had burst

As a community organizer in Chicago, Obama faced many challenges. His first victory came from his work at Altgeld Gardens (above in 2005), a housing project in the southern part of Chicago.

and toilets backed up. Broken windows marked many of the apartments that had been abandoned.

To begin, Obama posted flyers announcing a street corner meeting outside a nearby church. Those who came were invited to talk to their neighbors about the issues they complained about when they were in their homes. Eventually, the meetings were moved from the street corner outside the church to a larger gathering inside the church.

First, Obama focused on attracting jobs to the region. Big plants were moving further out into the suburbs, so Obama's group worked to attract smaller shops, restaurants, theaters, and services into the neighborhood—the kind of businesses that would provide entry-level jobs.

A full year passed before Obama began to experience some modest success. With the community's support, he was able to organize neighborhood cleanups, hold career days for the youth in the community, and bring pressure on a local politician to increase trash removal services. The Parks Department agreed to renovate rundown parks and playgrounds. Some streets were repaired, and crime-watch programs were started.

During this time, Obama also built a reputation for himself. Those who worked with him remember him as dedicated, hard-working, intelligent, inspiring, and a good listener. In David Moberg's April 2007 article in *The Nation,* one of the DCP board members, Loretta Augustine-Herron, described him as focused on doing things the right way. He would say, "Be open with the issues. Include the community instead of going behind the community's back. . . . You've got to bring people together. If you exclude people, you're only weakening yourself. If you meet behind doors and make decisions for them, they'll never take ownership of the issue."

One day, a resident of Altgeld came to a meeting and, as it ended, showed Obama a newspaper clipping. It was a small legal notice that had appeared in the classified section, seeking bids from contractors interested in a job removing asbestos from the management office of the Altgeld apartments.

Asbestos is a material that for many years was used in building construction to provide insulation and fireproofing. Eventually, scientists discovered that, when asbestos material is damaged or disturbed, the microscopic fibers that make up asbestos become airborne, causing significant health problems when they are inhaled, including certain types of cancer. For this reason, when asbestos is discovered in a building, it is often necessary to have it removed, which is an expensive process.

The presence of asbestos in the management office suggested that asbestos exposure might also be a problem in the apartments, but none of the residents had been notified of the possibility. When Obama and one of the residents met with the Altgeld manager, they were told that the apartments had been tested thoroughly and that no asbestos had been found. Their request for a copy of the test, however, resulted in several excuses and delays.

Finally, Obama and a small group of residents took a bus downtown to meet with the officials in their center-city office. They were not admitted until a group of reporters, armed with television cameras, arrived and began to film the scene. When the residents were allowed in, officials informed them that no testing had been done, but they promised that testing would begin by the end of that day. They would have a meeting with the director, and the date of that meeting was announced to the media.

Ultimately, the apartments were tested and the city was forced to clean them up. In *Dreams From My Father*, Obama noted that the bus ride downtown to demand action changed him in a fundamental way:

> It was the sort of change that's important not because it alters your concrete circumstances in some way (wealth, security, fame) but because it hints at what might be possible and therefore spurs you on, beyond the immediate exhilaration, beyond any subsequent disappointments, to retrieve that thing that you once, ever so briefly, held in your hand. That bus ride kept me going, I think. Maybe it still does.

The experiences Obama had as a community organizer would shape his views as a politician. Many of the themes from this work—an effort to find common ground among different viewpoints, a belief in ordinary citizens, a desire to examine issues and shape them into winnable positions—would resonate in his 2008 presidential campaign. One member of the DCP recruited by Obama, Reverend Alvin Love, said of the presidential candidate in a March 2007 *Chicago Tribune* article, "I think at his heart Barack is a community organizer. I think what he's doing now is that. It's just a larger community to be organized."

MEETING A SISTER

During this time, Auma, Obama's half-sister, visited from Kenya and shared stories of their father that helped clarify some of the mixed feelings Obama experienced upon learning of his father's death. Auma was older than Obama—she was born while their father was a student in Hawaii. At the time she and Obama met, she was a student in Germany studying for a master's degree in linguistics.

Auma filled in many of the pieces of Barack Obama Sr.'s life story that had always puzzled his son. She explained that she and their older brother, Roy, were four and six and living with their mother in the town of Alego when their father finally returned to Kenya from the United States, after completing his studies at Harvard. He returned with another American woman—a white woman named Ruth—and took his two children away from their mother to live with him and Ruth in Nairobi.

Ruth was the first white woman Auma had ever been near. Kenya had only recently gained its independence, and Barack Obama Sr. was hired to work for an American oil company. He soon became wealthy, purchased a large home and a large car, and talked politics while dining with his friends in the higher circles of the Kenyan government. He still claimed both Auma's mother and Ruth as his wives, and each woman bore him two more sons.

Barack Obama Sr. eventually left his job with the American oil company to work for the Kenyan government in the Ministry of Tourism, but at this point his success began to wane. There were divisions and rivalries between the different tribes in the government, and charges of corruption and protests soon followed.

Obama's father refused to keep silent. He was outspoken when he felt that he was being unfairly treated or that others less qualified were given promotions when he was not. He was eventually blacklisted, and found it impossible to find work in any government position. Foreign companies operating in Kenya were warned not to hire him, and when he finally was hired by a company in Ethiopia, his passport was revoked, preventing him from leaving Kenya.

Finally, a friend took pity on the elder Obama and gave him a minor job with the Water Department. He made barely enough to feed his family. The dramatic change in his fortune was a deep source of embarrassment to him, and he began to drink heavily. Former friends avoided him, knowing that they risked being blacklisted themselves if they were spotted with him. Many urged him to apologize, to see if a changed attitude would win back his favor with the government, but he refused.

Obama Sr. became abusive to his American wife, and she left, taking her two sons with her but leaving Auma and Roy behind. Their father was soon involved in a serious car accident, most likely caused by his drunken driving, and shortly after being released from the hospital, he traveled to Hawaii to spend that brief month with Barack. Before leaving, he told his children that he would come back with Barack and Barack's mother, but when he finally returned to Kenya, he was alone.

The car accident caused Obama to lose his job with the Water Department, and the family could no longer afford their home. They lived with various relatives and borrowed money for food. Roy eventually ran away, and Auma was granted a scholarship to a boarding school.

Eventually, the government in Kenya changed hands, and Barack's father once more was able to get a government job, this time with the Ministry of Finance. He never fully recovered from the bitterness of that earlier experience, however, according to Auma. He had one more son with another woman before he died.

The story provided a painful revelation to Obama. "I felt as if my world had been turned on its head," he recounted in *Dreams From My Father,*

> as if I had woken up to find a blue sun in the yellow sky, or heard animals speaking like men. All my life I had carried a single image of my father, one that I had sometimes rebelled against but had never questioned, one that I had later tried

to take as my own. The brilliant scholar, the generous friend, the upstanding leader—my father had been all those things. All those things and more, because except for that one brief visit in Hawaii, he had never been present to foil the image.

Obama struggled with the fact that the idealized image he had created of his father had been replaced by something else—a defeated man, an abusive husband, a drunk. There was a challenge in the empty space that had been created by this revelation. No longer did he have a ghost to try to live up to; instead he had to determine, on his own, what kind of man he wanted to be.

A NEW PATH

His sister's visit and her revelations about their father left Obama with a new kind of restlessness. He began to realize that he needed to do more with his life. Rather than simply help people find solutions to their problems, he wanted to be able to eliminate those problems altogether.

The experience of community organization had shaped him in a significant way. "I grew up to be a man, right here," he would later say at a convention of the still-active DCP. "It's as a consequence of working with this organization and this community that I found my calling. There was something more than making money and getting a fancy degree. The measure of my life would be public service."

Obama built a community not only in the neighborhood where he worked, but he also built a community for himself, a community with which he would maintain a relationship and an identity. In 1992, he worked from the DCP office to run a drive to register 150,000 new voters, and he used his ties to launch his grassroots campaign for the Illinois State Senate.

"I can't say we didn't make mistakes, that I knew what I was doing," Obama said of his work at the DCP, recounted in David Moberg's April 2007 article in *The Nation.* "Sometimes I called a meeting, and nobody showed up. Sometimes preachers said, 'Why should I listen to you?' Sometimes we tried to hold politicians accountable, and they didn't show up. I couldn't tell whether I got more out of it than this neighborhood."

A drive to do more, however, eventually led him to the realization that, in order to help eliminate the problems that were affecting the community, he would need a law degree. He felt that he needed to understand the way businesses and banks were put together, the legislative process, what made real estate ventures successful. He applied to three law schools—Harvard, Yale, and Stanford—and then set about establishing a new youth program, raising the following year's budget, and working to bring more churches into the organization. Then, he found someone to take his place and trained him.

He also found, in those final months, a church and a religious identity. He had first met with Reverend Jeremiah Wright, pastor of Chicago's Trinity United Church of Christ, as part of his effort to increase the number of churches working with DCP. Although he had worked with numerous ministers and churches in connection with his work, faith had not been a central part of his life. The meeting with Reverend Wright would soon change that.

Reverend Wright led a church that spoke of African history, worked actively to combat poverty, and focused on commitment to the black community and the black family. Members emphasized education, hard work, discipline, and self-respect. The church dedicated its resources to legal aid, tutoring sessions, and drug programs, all designed to support the needs of residents from nearby housing projects. The church's membership included people from all income brackets. The residents of the housing projects who were being helped sat next to members of the working class, engineers, doctors, and accountants.

As Obama met with several members of the church, he found a common theme—a theme that resonated with him. The church was also building a community. Obama remained a skeptic, however, until he finally chose to attend a service one Sunday morning. The title of Reverend Wright's sermon that day was "The Audacity of Hope." The minister spoke of the pain and hardships that members of the congregation would endure, the rejection and despair they would face. Then he spoke of hope, the hope that exists and that triumphs, a bold hope that unites communities and promises something more for those who believe.

The experience created a new understanding in Obama. He would later title one of his books *The Audacity of Hope* and would speak of how he came to realize the power of the black church to minister to the whole person, how faith could be "more than just a comfort to the weary or a hedge against death; rather it was an active, palpable agent in the world." Obama was moved by the message of Trinity United—that

IN HIS OWN WORDS...

On May 19, 2007, Barack Obama was invited to speak at the Southern New Hampshire University commencement. His remarks included a call to service that reflected his own work as a community organizer:

> There's a lot of talk in this country about the federal deficit. But I think we should talk more about our empathy deficit—the ability to put ourselves in someone else's shoes; to see the world through those who are different from us—the child who's hungry, the laid-off steelworker, the immigrant woman cleaning your dorm room.
>
> As you go on in life, cultivating this quality of empathy will become harder, not easier. There's no community service requirement in the real world; no one forcing you to care. You'll be free to live in neighborhoods with people who are exactly like yourself, and send your kids to the same schools, and narrow your concerns to what's going on in your own little circle.
>
> Not only that—we live in a culture that discourages empathy. A culture that too often tells us our principle goal in life is to be rich, thin, young,

faith meant being part of the world, actively serving and ministering to those in need:

> It was because of these newfound understandings—that religious commitment did not require me to suspend critical thinking, disengage from the battle for economic and social justice, or otherwise retreat from the world that I knew and loved—that I was finally able to walk down the aisle of Trinity United Church of Christ one day and be baptized.

Obama had spent many years as a skeptic, but the Trinity United Church of Christ became his spiritual home, a connection he would maintain even after leaving Chicago. Reverend Wright would later preside over Obama's wedding and baptize his two daughters.

famous, safe, and entertained. A culture where those in power too often encourage these selfish impulses.

They will tell you that the Americans who sleep in the streets and beg for food got there because they're all lazy or weak of spirit. That the inner-city children who are trapped in dilapidated schools can't learn and won't learn and so we should just give up on them entirely. That the innocent people being slaughtered and expelled from their homes half a world away are someone else's problem to take care of.

I hope you don't listen to this. I hope you choose to broaden, and not contract, your ambit of concern. Not because you have an obligation to those who are less fortunate, although you do have that obligation. Not because you have a debt to all of those who helped you get to where you are, although you do have that debt.

It's because you have an obligation to yourself. Because our individual salvation depends on collective salvation. And because it's only when you hitch your wagon to something larger than yourself that you will realize your true potential—and become full-grown.

6

Legal Training

Before beginning law school at Harvard, Obama traveled to Kenya to spend more time with his half-sister Auma and meet other members of his family. When he arrived at Jomo Kenyatta International Airport, he almost immediately felt a sense of belonging.

He wrote in *Dreams From My Father*, "No one here in Kenya would ask how to spell my name, or mangle it with an unfamiliar tongue. My name belonged and so I belonged, drawn into a web of relationships, alliances, and grudges that I did not yet understand."

Obama spent time with Auma in Nairobi, where she was teaching at the university. He met his father's family, and heard stories of his father as a boy and a young man. He met his father's first wife, who greeted him saying, "My other son has come home." He went on safari, and traveled to Kisumu, to the place where his grandmother lived, to find his father's

Obama poses on the campus of Harvard Law School. Obama's tenure at Harvard would mark the beginning of his career in the public eye. When he became the first black editor of the Harvard Law Review, the *New York Times* profiled him, and he was later commissioned to write his memoirs.

Harvard diploma still proudly displayed on the wall. There were copies of more than 30 letters—the letters his father had sent to various colleges in the United States seeking admission. And there, behind his grandmother's home, were two smooth yellow tiles, marking the place where his father and grand-father were buried. There was joy for Obama in the trip—in discovering much of what had been missing from his sense of self—and new understanding that came from the stories he heard of his father.

LAW SCHOOL

Obama attended law school from 1988 to 1991. It was a period that marked the start of Obama's career in the public eye. By the time he left law school, he had been profiled in the *New York Times* and received a book contract for his memoirs.

At 27, Obama was one of the older students at the prestigious law school. He was quieter than many of his fellow students and was well liked for his habit of trying to create consensus among different viewpoints, as well as for being a good listener. His grades were good, and as a result, and because of a well-written essay submitted for a writing competition, he was one of 40 students awarded a spot on the *Harvard Law Review*, one of the most powerful legal journals in the country.

The *Law Review* is a student-run legal journal that provides students with a chance to publish their legal research and writing and gives judges and legal scholars a place to find new legal arguments. Among similar publications, the *Harvard Law Review* is considered the most prestigious.

In the summer after his first year of law school, Obama returned to Chicago. He had been hired as a summer associate by Sidley & Austin, a large corporate law firm based in Chicago. Obama initially wrestled with the decision to work in corporate law. His plan was to return to do some form of community organizing when he completed law school, and he felt guilty at working in a fancy law office, when so many of his friends were still working in Chicago's poorest neighborhoods. He needed the money to pay for school, however.

As he recounted in *The Audacity of Hope*, Obama rented the cheapest apartment he could find, purchased the first three suits he would ever own and a pair of shoes that turned out to be a half size too small. On his first day, he was told to report to the office of the young attorney who had been assigned to serve as his summer adviser. Michelle Robinson was three years younger than Obama, but because she had gone to Harvard directly after college, she was already working as a lawyer.

Obama writes of his first impression of the woman who would become his wife: she was tall "and lovely—with a friendly, professional manner that matched her tailored suit and blouse." She explained some of the details of the work that Obama would be doing and how the firm operated. Over lunch, she told him a bit about herself—that she had grown up on Chicago's South Side, just a short distance from the communities where Obama had organized. She had attended Princeton as an undergraduate, and specialized in entertainment law.

For several weeks she refused to date Obama, but finally agreed to an ice cream cone at Baskin-Robbins. They soon

On Race

In *The Audacity of Hope*, Barack Obama acknowledged that his experiences with racism, although in some ways unique, provided him with a strong commitment to use his position to illuminate how race impacts America:

> To think clearly about race, then, requires us to see the world on a split screen—to maintain in our sights the kind of America that we want while looking squarely at America as it is, to acknowledge the sins of our past and the challenges of the present without becoming trapped in cynicism or despair. I have witnessed a profound shift in race relations in my lifetime. I have felt it as surely as one feels a change in the temperature. When I hear some in the black community deny those changes, I think it not only dishonors those who struggled on our behalf but also robs us of our agency to complete the work they began. But as much as I insist that things have gotten better, I am mindful of this truth as well: Better isn't good enough.

**In the summer after his first year at Harvard, Obama went
to work at the Chicago law firm of Sidley & Austin. There,
he met Michelle Robinson, an attorney who was assigned to
supervise him for the summer. Later, Obama and Robinson
would marry. Michelle Obama, pictured above in 2007, is
her husband's staunchest advocate.**

were spending more and more time together. Obama met her
family. He loved the sense of belonging that he experienced in
her home and he was impressed by her parents. Six months
after meeting Michelle, he stood by her side when she buried

her father. Obama returned to Harvard no longer interested in dating other people, but focused on completing his studies and returning to Chicago.

HARVARD LAW REVIEW

In his second year, Obama was urged by friends to run for the presidency of the *Law Review.* "It's an election among a closed group," former *Review* editor Bruce Spiva said in a 2007 *New York Times* article. "It's more like electing a pope." Obama at first refused to compete for the presidency, but finally agreed.

Obama was one of 19 candidates competing for the position, and the 80 editors of the *Law Review* spent all day meeting with the various candidates in large groups, testing their intellectual and social skills and then eliminating them, several at a time. Partisan differences marked the various competing forces backing different candidates. When the conservative candidate was defeated, the conservative backers decided to support Obama. "Whatever his politics, we felt he would give us a fair shake," Bradford Berenson (who would go on to serve in the administration of President George W. Bush) told a reporter.

It was this reputation for fairness and for an ability to build consensus among different viewpoints that helped place Obama in the final round, one of two candidates for the position. Finally, Obama was declared the winner, and he became the first black president of the prestigious law journal in its 104-year history.

The event drew the attention of national media. Obama was quoted in the *New York Times* in February 1990. He was already exercising a talent that would serve him well in future political races. "The fact that I've been elected shows a lot of progress," he said. "It's encouraging. But it's important that stories like mine aren't used to say that everything is O.K. for blacks. You have to remember that for every one of me, there are hundreds or thousands of black students with at least equal talent who don't get a chance."

Obama promised to make the *Law Review* a "forum for debate," to bring in new writers and make the writing livelier and more accessible. He told *New York Times* reporter Fox Butterfield, "I personally am interested in pushing a strong minority perspective. I'm fairly opinionated about this. But as president of the law review, I have a limited role as only first among equals."

Many view serving as president of the *Law Review* as a step to other prestigious positions. The *Law Review* president often goes on to serve as a clerk for a judge on the Federal Court of Appeals for a year and then becomes a clerk for an associate justice of the Supreme Court. Obama was clear that his career path would be a different one, however. He planned to spend two or three years in private law practice before returning to Chicago, either to work as a community organizer or to enter politics. The attention Obama received led to a book contract for his memoirs. Obama made notes for the book that would be published as *Dreams From My Father* a few years later.

Once some of the attention died down, though, Obama was faced with the challenge of balancing class work with the demands of the *Law Review*. There was infighting among the editors, sparked by different political views. Obama had to decide whether to accept or reject articles by some of the law school's most well-known professors. There were arguments over affirmative action and racial issues affecting the campus.

Obama's approach was to insist that labels mattered less than real-life issues. In speeches, he reminded his fellow students how privileged they were to be attending Harvard Law School and urged them to honor the responsibilities that came with that education. He shared the details of his background, his life story, to prove that his rise to the presidency of the *Law Review* had not been an easy or obvious process. He completed his work at the *Law Review* and graduated with high honors from Harvard Law School in 1991.

As editor of the *Law Review*, Obama promised to make the journal a "forum for debate." But first, he had to face debate among his own editorial staff—infighting was common because of differences in political views.

TEACHER AND ACTIVIST

Obama honored his pledge to return to Chicago. He began a drive to register voters for the 1992 elections, ultimately registering more than 100,000 voters. He solicited financial support for the drive from many of Chicago's most prominent Democratic contributors and built contacts among Chicago's successful black executives and entrepreneurs. Many of these men and women would support Obama when he chose to run for office. On a personal note, Obama married Michelle Robinson in 1992 and worked on his book, which was published in 1995.

Obama had many big-money offers from large law firms, but instead he chose to accept a position with the small law firm of Miner, Barnhill & Galland, which specialized in civil rights and housing discrimination cases for low-income clients. He also took a part-time job teaching constitutional law at the University of Chicago. He loved his teaching, and he noted his appreciation for the moment when the Constitution became accessible for his students, "a part not just of the past but of their present and their future."

In 1996, at age 37, Obama decided to enter politics with a run for the Illinois State Senate. He won and traveled to Springfield to take his place in the legislature.

7

Illinois State Senator

Although a group of friends urged Obama to run for an open seat in the Illinois state legislature, he had actually been considering a move into politics for several years. In *Dreams From My Father,* Obama described the work as

> satisfying, mostly because the scale of state politics allows for concrete results—an expansion of health insurance for poor children, or a reform of laws that send innocent men to death row—within a meaningful time frame. And too, because within the capitol building of a big, industrial state, one sees every day the face of a nation in constant conversation: inner-city mothers and corn and bean farmers, immigrant day laborers alongside suburban investment bankers—all jostling to be heard, all ready to tell their stories.

Obama would go on to serve in the Illinois state legislature from 1997 to 2004. While there, he was a member of the Committee on Health and Human Services (serving as its chairperson), the Judiciary Committee, the Committee on Local Government, and the Committee on Welfare. He focused on welfare legislation and the earned income tax credit. His work on behalf of the tax credit helped result, over a three-year period, in more than $100 million in tax cuts for families throughout Illinois. Another key issue for Obama was expanding early childhood education.

Obama worked to pass a statute requiring the videotaping of interrogations and confessions in homicide cases, despite the opposition of prosecutors, who argued that the electronic recording would be expensive and cumbersome. The newly elected Democratic governor of Illinois had declared his opposition to the videotaping of interrogations during his campaign, and Obama risked being labeled as "soft on crime" for his stance.

Obama's solution was to bring together in regular meetings representatives from the prosecutors' offices, public defenders, members of police organizations, and representatives lobbying to strike down the death penalty. These meetings were convened quietly and in private, and Obama wisely focused not on the death penalty but instead on the desire to keep innocent people off death row and to ensure that the guilty were caught and punished. "When police representatives presented concrete problems with the bill's design that would have impeded their investigations, we modified the bill," he later wrote in *The Audacity of Hope.*

> When police representatives offered to videotape only confessions, we held firm, pointing out that the whole purpose of the bill was to give the public confidence that confessions were obtained free of coercion. At the end of the process, the bill had the support of all the parties involved.

Obama served in the Illinois state legislature from 1997 to 2004. Above, he confers with Illinois Senate president Emil Jones on the Senate floor during a session at the state capitol in Springfield, Illinois.

It passed unanimously in the Illinois Senate and was signed into law.

There were frustrations as well as successes. His bill to provide school breakfasts to preschoolers was defeated. For six of his eight years in the state Senate, he and his fellow Democrats were the minority in a Republican-controlled Senate, making it difficult for Democratic-sponsored bills to be signed into law.

Even in the political minority, though, Obama's work was often critical, in part because of his willingness to build consensus by crossing party lines to obtain the support of Republican colleagues. "He was looked upon by members of both parties as someone whose view we listened carefully to," Republican state senator Kirk Dillard told CBS News in January 2007. "He was passionate in his views," state senator Dave Syverson, a Republican committee chairman who worked on welfare reform with Obama, noted in Joe Klein's *Time* interview. "We had some pretty fierce arguments. We went round and round about how much to spend on day care, for example. But he was not your typical party-line politician. A lot of Democrats didn't want to have any work requirement at all for people on welfare. Barack was willing to make that deal."

Obama was often forced to take positions on critical issues. In the State Senate, he supported abortion rights and family planning services. He supported gun-control measures, including a ban on semiautomatic "assault weapons" and a limit on handgun purchases to one per month. He argued that people charged with violating local handgun bans after using their guns in their homes should not be allowed to use self-defense as an excuse. He and fellow Democrats alleged that the measure could open loopholes that would allow gun owners who used their weapons on the street to claim self-defense, too. Despite his opposition, however, the bill passed 41–16 and became state law.

Although he was generally a proponent of gun control, Obama did support a measure to let retired police officers and military police carry concealed weapons. He also joined his fellow Democrats in an effort to solve a budget deficit by raising more than 300 taxes and fees on businesses in 2004, an effort that passed in the Senate 30–28.

By 2004, Obama and the other Democrats controlled the Senate. Obama played a key role in many efforts during the final two years of his service in the state legislature. He continued his efforts to overhaul the capital punishment system and played an important role in requiring a study of traffic stops across the state to search for signs of racial profiling.

Barack and Michelle Obama have two daughters: Malia, born in 1999, and Natasha, born in 2001. Above, the Obama family spends time together in their hotel suite on the eve of the 2004 U.S. Senate Democratic primary. Obama was elected to the Senate later that year.

His commitments to the poor and to equal rights were clearly reflected in many of his legislative actions. He voted to raise the minimum wage and passed a 5 percent earned-income tax credit for low-income working families. He voted to end certain tax breaks for businesses and cosponsored a prescription drug discount buying-club program for senior citizens and the disabled.

He sponsored legislation to bar job and housing discrimination against gays. He voted to have Illinois endorse embryonic stem cell research and sponsored the Health Care Justice Act, a study of ways to implement a universal healthcare system in Illinois. He successfully cosponsored an ethics reform bill, and voted against giving tax credits to parents who send their children to private school.

CONGRESSIONAL RACE

All this was the result of some eight years in the state Senate. Those years, however, also included the births of his daughter Malia in 1999 and his daughter Natasha in 2001.

Obama's first political defeat was an unsuccessful run for the U.S. Congress in 2000. "It was a race in which everything that could go wrong did go wrong, in which my own mistakes were compounded by tragedy and farce," Obama wrote in *The Audacity of Hope.*

In that campaign, Obama challenged the incumbent South Side Democrat Bobby Rush in the primary for the Illinois First Congressional District seat. Rush, a former Black Panther, was well known throughout Chicago. Two weeks after announcing his candidacy, Obama commissioned his first poll and learned that his name recognition stood at a mere 11 percent, whereas Rush's was 90 percent. Rush's approval rating was 70 percent; Obama's only 8 percent.

These were devastating numbers for a campaign that had only raised a few thousand dollars at that point. The campaign further struggled when Congressman Rush's adult son was shot and killed by drug dealers outside his home. Out of respect for the loss his opponent had suffered, Obama chose to suspend his campaign for a month.

Over the Christmas holidays that year, Obama, his wife, and then-18-month-old Malia traveled to Hawaii to spend a few days with his grandmother. His daughter became ill, and when the state legislature was called back into special session to vote on a piece of gun control legislation, he chose to remain in Hawaii. The bill failed to pass by only a few votes, and Obama was skewered in the press for choosing to remain "on vacation" while a critical piece of gun control legislation was being debated.

Obama won the endorsement of the *Chicago Tribune* and received some favorable press for his proposals on education and health care. Before the campaign was even half over, though, he had a clear sense that he was going to lose. "Each morning from that point forward I awoke with a vague sense of dread, realizing that I would have to spend the day smil-

Bobby Rush

Barack Obama's first attempt at a statewide political race was unsuccessful. In 2000, he challenged incumbent Congressman Bobby Rush in the Democratic primary and lost.

Bobby Rush was born in Georgia in 1946, and grew up in Chicago's North Side (although it was the South Side he would represent in Congress). He served in the U.S. Army and became active in the civil rights movement in the 1960s. In 1967, he founded the Chicago chapter of the Black Panthers, a militant organization that called for the arming of African Americans, their exemption from military service, and compensation payments for the years African Americans had suffered under slavery. Rush survived a police raid of a Black Panther meeting in 1969 during which two of the group's leaders were killed.

Rush successfully coordinated a medical clinic that offered testing for sickle-cell anemia but was imprisoned for six months in 1972 on a weapons charge. He later earned a college degree and a master's degree in theology. He left the Panthers in 1974.

In 1983, Rush was elected alderman in Chicago's South Side, his first elected office, and he quickly became an effective political organizer, delivering large voter turnouts for himself and the candidates he supported. In 1992 he was elected to Congress in the Illinois First District, ultimately gaining a seat on the powerful Commerce Committee, which he used as a forum to encourage increased black ownership of businesses.

He waged an unsuccessful campaign to become mayor of Chicago in 1999 but then turned his focus back to Congress, serving eight successive terms in the House of Representatives.

Obama's first attempt at a statewide political race, in which he challenged the incumbent, Congressman Bobby Rush, was unsuccessful. Rush, pictured above, was a member of the Black Panthers in the 1960s and early 1970s; he would also serve as an alderman in Chicago before being elected to Congress in 1992.

ing and shaking hands and pretending that everything was going according to plan," he wrote in *The Audacity of Hope*. Rush defeated him soundly, winning 61 percent of the vote to Obama's 30 percent.

Obama returned to the State Senate with newfound wisdom about campaigning on a larger stage. When his daughter Malia was diagnosed with chronic asthma, his focus on environmental issues increased, inspiring his support for legislation combating smog and air pollution. He took an aggressive stance to combat pollution from Illinois coal plants, a leading producer of the state's electricity. He met with officials in the coal-mining industry to brainstorm ways in which better pollution controls on power plants could create new markets for Illinois coal. He sponsored a measure to require 10 percent of the electricity generated in Illinois to come from renewable sources by 2012 and supported another bill to tighten energy-efficiency codes in residential and commercial buildings.

His environmental efforts also focused on boosting fuel economy standards on cars, imposing tougher standards on diesel engines, and battling urban sprawl and the destruction of Illinois wetlands. He received high rankings from the Sierra Club and other environmental organizations for his position on environmental issues.

RACE FOR THE SENATE

By the fall of 2002, Obama felt that he had accomplished all that he had set out to do in the state legislature and was eager to try to run for a higher office again. This time his choice was the race for the U.S. Senate.

In October 2002, knowing that he would soon announce his decision to run for the U.S. Senate, Obama received an invitation from a group of Chicago activists to speak at a rally protesting the expected U.S. invasion of Iraq. At the time, intelligence reports seemed to indicate that Iraq possessed so-called "weapons of mass destruction" that could threaten U.S. security. President George W. Bush had strong public support—and the support of the Senate—for a planned invasion.

It was clear that an outspoken position against the actions of a popular president at a time when the security of the U.S. was threatened could prove politically disastrous for Obama's campaign. Obama believed that the people of Iraq would be better off without their leader, Saddam Hussein. He assumed from the intelligence reports that Iraq possessed chemical and biological weapons; in the past Hussein had used them against his own people.

Obama felt that Hussein's threat was not an imminent one, however, and distrusted the reasons the Bush Administration gave for the war. He felt that diplomatic options had not yet been exhausted and that the United States needed first to build a broader international support for the invasion.

So, Obama agreed to speak at the rally. Before some 2,000 people in the heart of Chicago, he delivered a speech that would prove astonishingly full of foresight in years to come. "I

IN HIS OWN WORDS...

In *The Audacity of Hope*, Barack Obama expressed his belief that certain core values unite all Americans:

"We hold these truths to be self-evident, that all men are created equal, that they are endowed by their Creator with certain unalienable Rights, that among these are Life, Liberty and the pursuit of Happiness."

Those simple words are our starting point as Americans; they describe not only the foundation of our government but the substance of our common creed. Not every American may be able to recite them; few, if asked, could trace the genesis of the Declaration of Independence to its roots in eighteenth-century liberal and republican thought. But the essential idea behind the Declaration—that we are born into this world free, all of us; that each of us arrives with a bundle of rights that can't be taken away by any person or any state without just cause; that through our own agency we can, and must, make of our lives what we will—is one that every American understands. It orients us, sets our course, each and every day.

know that even a successful war against Iraq will require a U.S. occupation of undetermined length, at undetermined cost, with undetermined consequences," he said. "I know that an invasion of Iraq without a clear rationale and without strong international support will only fan the flames of the Middle East, and encourage the worst, rather than the best, impulses of the Arab world, and strengthen the recruitment arm of Al Qaeda."

The speech won him strong support in a challenging campaign, but Obama was one of seven Democrats vying for a primary win. One of his opponents was far wealthier; another was the "official" candidate of the Illinois Democratic Party. It would take a combination of luck and skill for him to win the primary and an astonishing appearance on the national stage to transform him into a political star.

8

Campaign for the U.S. Senate

The first step in Obama's campaign for the U.S. Senate was to raise millions of dollars to finance his effort. This was not an easy task. When Obama began his campaign, he was still paying off the $20,000 in debt he had incurred from his unsuccessful congressional campaign.

Obama targeted a group of key donors, including members of Chicago's black professional class, as well as friends from Harvard Law School and the University of Chicago. He was not comfortable asking for money, but understood that it was an important part of the process in seeking elective office.

According to a *New York Times* article by Christopher Drew and Mike McIntire, Steven S. Rogers, a former business owner who teaches at Northwestern University's Kellogg School of Management, played golf with Obama in 2001. "By the sixth hole, [Obama] said, 'Steve, I want to run for the Senate.' And by the ninth hole, he said he needed help to clear up some debts."

Obama ultimately raised more than $5 million for the primary alone—and that amount came from just 300 donors. For the Senate campaign, he raised $15 million in total. Many agreed to support his campaign after meeting him.

Still, some of his friends urged him to wait when he initially announced his decision to enter the Senate race. They felt it was too soon after his unsuccessful congressional campaign and that the competition among Democrats was too stiff. The Democratic candidates included the state comptroller (whose family had strong ties to the state Democratic Party), a multimillionaire businessman, Chicago Mayor Richard Daley's former chief of staff, and a black female healthcare professional. Obama seemed the least likely candidate to win the party's nomination—he generally came in third or fourth in name recognition among the candidates.

Obama hired four young staffers to manage his campaign and often spent four to five hours a day calling donors for contributions. He requested a spot in Chicago's annual St. Patrick's Day parade and was placed at the very end, marching only steps in front of the garbage trucks assigned to clean up the parade route.

Obama traveled across Illinois, going wherever friends or contacts had invited him, meeting prospective voters in someone's home, a church, or at a bridge club. There were times when he would drive several hours to find only two or three people waiting to meet him. Obama wrote in *The Audacity of Hope* that his focus at these gatherings was on listening as much as talking:

> Most of them thought that anybody willing to work should be able to find a job that paid a living wage. They figured that people shouldn't have to file for bankruptcy because they got sick. They believed that every child should have a genuinely good education—that it shouldn't just be a bunch of talk—and those same children should be able to go to

college even if their parents weren't rich. They wanted to be
safe, from criminals and from terrorists; they wanted clean
air, clean water, and time with their kids. And when they got
old, they wanted to be able to retire with some dignity and
respect.

These conversations inspired Obama, reminding him of
his work as a community organizer and why he had chosen to
enter politics in the first place. He believed that politics revolved
around priorities, and that a shift in government's priorities
could ensure a better life for the families he was meeting.

ON THE CAMPAIGN TRAIL

As the primary drew nearer, polls conducted by Obama's campaign revealed that prospective voters—especially suburban
women—were responding positively whenever he shared his
life story. Without knowing much about his accomplishments
as a state senator or his positions on the issues, voters liked
him when they heard about his background. Writer Benn Wallace-Wells described it as the equivalent of Abraham Lincoln's
log cabin. Throughout American history, candidates have
used real or manufactured stories of their background to help
distinguish them from their opponents and to connect with
voters. Obama's story was unique and presented voters with a
different picture of the candidate.

Obama began to share his life story on the campaign trail,
talking about his white mother from Kansas and his African
father. In addition to his accomplishments in the state legislature, Obama discussed his life in Indonesia and his experiences
with racism in Hawaii.

Despite some successes, Obama seemed likely to lose to
businessman Blair Hull, who spent some $29 million of his
own money on the race. Hull's campaign collapsed only weeks
before the primary, though, when the press obtained copies

When Obama noticed that prospective voters responded positively to his life story, he began telling his story while on the campaign trail. His autobiography, *Dreams from My Father*, originally published in 1995, was reissued. The cover above is from the first edition.

of his divorce records, which revealed his wife's accusations of violent behavior.

In March 2004, when the primary was held, Obama staged an upset, winning more than 52 percent of the vote statewide. His closest opponent was State Comptroller Dan Hynes, who received less than 24 percent.

According to a *New York Times* article by Monica Savey, when the results were announced, an overjoyed Obama told a ballroom of supporters:

> We didn't have enough money. We didn't have enough organization. There was no way that a skinny guy from the South Side with a funny name like Barack Obama could ever win a statewide race. Sixteen months later we are here, and Democrats from all across Illinois—suburbs, city, downstate, upstate, black, white, Hispanic, Asian—have declared: Yes, we can! Yes, we can! Yes, we can!

IN THE SPOTLIGHT

Obama's upset victory in the primary inspired immediate national interest. The Senate seat in Illinois had been targeted by Democrats, who desperately wanted to win it back from the Republicans. If Obama won the general election, he would become the Senate's only black member.

Obama's Republican opponent was Jack Ryan, a wealthy former business executive who had give up a lucrative career to become an inner-city teacher. Ryan was vying with Obama for the seat that had been held by another Republican, Peter Fitzgerald, who had chosen not to run for reelection. Ryan quickly launched a campaign attacking Obama, but before he could capitalize on it, he too faced a divorce scandal and was ultimately forced to step out of the race.

Once more, luck played a role in Obama's efforts to seek the Senate seat. As Republicans scrambled to find someone to run against Obama, he spent several weeks traveling Illinois without any kind of serious opposition. The national media continued to cover his efforts, aware of the historical context for this race: There had been only two black members of the Senate since Reconstruction, and one of them, Carol Moseley Braun, had been from Illinois.

Obama was invited to speak at a fund-raiser for John Kerry, who had recently received the Democratic nomination for the presidency and was campaigning hard against his Republican opponent, President George W. Bush, who was seeking a second term in office. Obama spoke at the Illinois fund-raiser and then went with Kerry to another campaign event that focused on job-training programs. It was the first time he had met Kerry, so Obama was a bit surprised when, a few weeks later, he was invited by Kerry to speak at the 2004 Democratic Convention, which was being held in Boston in July. Later, Obama learned that, not only was he invited to speak at the Convention, he was in fact scheduled to deliver the keynote address. Apart from the speeches given by the presidential and vice-presidential candidates, the keynote address is one of the most visible in the convention and is scheduled to attract maximum television viewers and set the tone for the convention.

Obama had been to only one other Democratic Convention—the 2000 convention held in Los Angeles. That trip had been a disaster. He had been persuaded by friends to attend at the last minute. His credit card was rejected at the car rental company at the Los Angeles airport. Finally, he was unable to get a floor pass and so ended up watching the speech on a television screen before finally flying back to Chicago.

KEYNOTE ADDRESS

On July 27, 2004, Barack Obama introduced himself to a national television audience, in one of the most memorable moments in the 2004 presidential race. Although the aim of his speech was to urge those listening to vote for the Democratic candidate, John Kerry, the speech ultimately prompted many to wonder when Barack Obama himself would be a presidential candidate.

The theme of Obama's speech was "the audacity of hope," the phrase taken from the sermon he had heard many years ago. Obama shared his life story, the story of a grandfather who had been a domestic servant and a father who was raised in a small village in Kenya. He told of his mother's father, who had been a G.I. in World War II, and her mother, who had worked on a bomber (a type of military airplane) assembly line.

His speech was a call to action, painting a picture of an America where dreams could be realized, where people deserved a chance to make their lives better. In one of the most memorable sections of his speech, he criticized those who sought to divide the country:

> Well, I say to them tonight, there's not a liberal America and a conservative America—there's the United States of America. There's not a black America and white America and Latino America and Asian America; there's the United States of America. The pundits like to slice-and-dice our country into Red States and Blue States; Red States for Republicans, Blue States for Democrats. But I've got news for them, too. We worship an awesome God in the Blue States, and we don't like federal agents poking around our libraries in the Red States. We coach Little League in the Blue States and have gay friends in the Red States. There are patriots who opposed the war in Iraq and patriots who supported it. We are one people, all of us pledging allegiance to the stars and stripes, all of us defending the United States of America.

In the 18 minutes he spoke before the Democratic National Convention, Obama was transformed from a Democratic candidate for the Senate to a political star. Suddenly, Obama was the person other Democratic candidates called—asking him to help them with fund-raising or to speak at their campaign rallies. Obama spoke at rallies for Russell Feingold, a 12-year veteran of the U.S. Senate seeking reelection in Wisconsin. He spoke at Democratic fund-raisers in Los Angeles and Denver. His own fund-raising efforts took off, so that his campaign was able to make contributions to the Democratic Senatorial Campaign Committee and to Democratic state parties with competitive races, including those in Alaska, Oklahoma, Wisconsin, Colorado, Florida, Kentucky, and South Dakota.

Illinois Republican party leaders began searching around for someone—anyone—to challenge Obama for the Senate

2004 Democratic Convention Keynote Address

On July 27, 2004, Barack Obama delivered the keynote address at the Democratic National Convention. His speech introduced him to a national audience and would prove the launching point for a presidential campaign three years later:

Do we participate in a politics of cynicism or a politics of hope? . . . I'm not talking about blind optimism here—the almost willful ignorance that thinks unemployment will go away if we just don't talk about it, or the health care crisis will solve itself if we just ignore it. No, I'm talking about something more substantial. It's the hope of slaves sitting around a fire singing freedom songs; the hope of immigrants setting out for distant shores; the hope of a young naval lieutenant bravely patrolling the Mekong Delta; the hope of a mill worker's son who dares to defy the odds; the hope of a skinny kid with a funny name who believes that America has a place for him, too. The audacity of hope!

In the end, that is God's greatest gift to us, the bedrock of this nation; the belief in things not seen; the belief that there are better days ahead. I believe we can give our middle class relief and provide working families with a road to opportunity. I believe we can provide jobs to the jobless, homes to the homeless, and reclaim young people in cities across America from violence and despair. I believe that as we stand on the crossroads of history, we can make the right choices, and meet the challenges that face us.

Conservative Alan Keyes (right) was a late entrant to the U.S. Senate race, challenging Obama in a campaign that was often confrontational.

seat. They finally settled on an unlikely choice: Alan Keyes, a political activist who lived in Maryland. He had twice run for the Senate in Maryland (in 1988 and 1992) and had twice sought the Republican nomination for the presidency (in 1996 and 2000). An African American with conservative credentials, Keyes had served in the administration of President Ronald Reagan and spent several years working in the State Department and the United Nations.

Keyes quickly rented an apartment outside Chicago and, according to Davey, began to campaign against Obama, dismissing his sudden fame as "manufactured, artificial hype like the Wizard of Oz." Keyes trailed by wide margins in the polls, but Obama writes in *The Audacity of Hope* that Keyes' confrontational campaign style managed to get under his skin, as did his comment that Jesus would never vote for Barack

Obama. "When our paths crossed during the campaign, I often had to suppress the rather uncharitable urge to either taunt him or wring his neck," Obama later wrote in *The Audacity of Hope.*

Obama's lead remained consistent throughout the final months of the campaign, however. In November 2004, he was elected to the U.S. Senate, capturing 70 percent of the vote.

9

The Senator From Illinois

The national attention—and suggestions that he should seek the presidency—continued as Obama assumed his position as the junior senator from Illinois. Obama dismissed these suggestions whenever reporters pressed him. He insisted that he had a job to do in the Senate and, according to Ben Wallace-Wells in *Rolling Stone,* his plan was simple: "Put Illinois first." He rented a one-bedroom apartment a few blocks from the Capitol. (He and Michelle had decided that she and the children would remain in Chicago.)

Obama was sworn in on January 4, 2005, and during his first months in Washington, he focused on learning the job of senator. He hired a staff and set up an office. He negotiated with other senators to get committee assignments and then gathered information on the issues pending before those committees. His early focus was on minor but important pieces of legislation: a plan to make it easier for citizens to find out about government spending, increasing research into alternative fuel sources such as ethanol, more job training and tax credits for fathers trying to care for families.

He decorated his office with pictures of the people he admired: Nelson Mandela, Abraham Lincoln, Martin Luther King Jr., John F. Kennedy, Mahatma Gandhi, Thurgood Marshall, and Muhammad Ali. Along with Richard Durbin, the senior senator from Illinois, he began hosting Constituent Coffees, where visitors from Illinois could meet and ask questions of the two men. Back in Illinois, he hosted town hall meetings, holding 39 of them during his first year in the Senate. Obama was a powerful draw at these meetings. Many who attended expressed their belief that they were seeing a future president of the United States.

Obama was appointed to several prestigious Senate committees, including the Foreign Relations Committee, the Veterans' Affairs Committee, and the Health, Education, Labor and Pensions Committee. In 2005 and 2006, he also served on the Environment and Public Works Committee.

IN HIS OWN WORDS...

In *The Audacity of Hope*, Barack Obama reflected on the pressure he felt, as a U.S. senator, to carefully measure his words:

In an environment in which a single ill-considered remark can generate more bad publicity than years of ill-considered policies, it should have come as no surprise to me that on Capitol Hill jokes got screened, irony became suspect, spontaneity was frowned upon, and passion was considered downright dangerous. I started to wonder how long it took for a politician to internalize all this; how long before the committee of scribes and editors and censors took residence in your head; how long before even the "candid" moments became scripted, so that you choked up or expressed outrage only on cue. How long before you started sounding like a politician?

Much of the legislation Obama sponsored reflected actions he had taken in Illinois while serving in the state legislature. He lobbied for more ethical government, for affordable health care, and for quality education from prekindergarten through college for all Americans. On his Senate Web page, he listed certain key issues: tax reform, good government, responsible spending, a new national energy policy, a redeployment of American troops in Iraq to bring the conflict to an end, defense capabilities, support for senior citizens, a sustainable environmental policy, focus on homeland security, a sensible immigration policy, and support for veterans. He visited Ethiopia and returned urging increased U.S. investments in the region. He secured funds to fight avian flu and improve security in the Congo.

When Hurricane Katrina struck and devastated New Orleans, Obama was contacted by the media for his thoughts on the government's poor response to the disaster. He toured the devastated region with two former presidents, Bill Clinton and George H.W. Bush. He traveled to Africa and was surrounded by crowds and media. In 2006, his second book was published. *The Audacity of Hope* offered his prescription for what he called "a new kind of politics, one that can excavate and build upon those shared understandings that pull us together as Americans."

Obama seldom took a position that put him too much at odds with the Democratic Party, yet he showed a willingness to work with conservative colleagues on issues he supported. He worked with a Republican senator from Pennsylvania, Rick Santorum, to support a bill providing funds for research on the effect of video games on brain development in children. He traveled to Russia, Ukraine, and Azerbaijan, working with Republican senator Richard Lugar to learn about efforts to dispose of nuclear weapons from the former Soviet Union.

Obama sounded a more liberal note, however, when he voted against the nomination of John Roberts to serve as chief justice of the U.S. Supreme Court, expressing his concerns about Roberts's votes on civil rights and abortion issues. He also opposed a proposal that would require photo identification for people to vote, expressing his concern that it might prevent poorer citizens, who did not have driver's licenses or passports, from voting.

THE NEXT RACE

The murmurs about Obama as a presidential candidate had been heard ever since the overwhelming response to his keynote address at the 2004 Democratic National Convention, but the buzz increased as Obama published his book *The Audacity of Hope*. The media attention and the public response came not only because of what Obama had accomplished, but also because of the idea of who he was and what he could be.

"I realized I didn't feel comfortable standing on the sidelines when so much was at stake," Obama told a reporter for *Rolling Stone*. "It was hard to maintain the notion that I was a backbencher." Instead, Obama began seriously exploring what a presidential race would involve. He made calls to prominent Democrats, met with labor activists and fundraisers, and traveled to New Hampshire, the traditional first state in the presidential primaries.

Long before Obama officially declared his intention to enter the race, an Internet-based "draft Obama" movement gathered 15,000 signatures and began to run ads in New Hampshire and Iowa, promoting his candidacy and begging him to run. People who wanted to work on his presidential campaign sent in resumes. His book steadily rose on the bestseller list.

Some also criticized Obama with a pointedness that had been rare in the early years of his political career. Questions were raised about Obama's relationship with Chicago developer Tony Rezko, who had contributed to Obama's campaign and with whom he entered into a legal but complicated real estate transaction. Rezko was under federal investigation at the time of the real-estate transaction and was later indicted.

After Hurricane Katrina struck New Orleans in September 2005, Obama toured the region along with two former presidents, Bill Clinton (left) and George H.W. Bush (right).

Obama was forced to publicly apologize for his involvement with Rezko.

In New Hampshire, Obama tested the waters, weaving his own personal story into discussions of what he felt government needed to focus on—increased spending on health care and education, energy independence, and an emphasis on improving relations with other countries. Crowds responded enthusiastically to his message. "I think what's going on is people are very hungry for something new; they are interested in being called to something larger," Obama told the reporters who had gathered to cover his trip.

On January 16, 2007, Obama announced his decision to form an exploratory committee to determine whether or not he should enter the 2008 presidential race. The announcement of the formation of the exploratory committee signaled to many that the decision making was over: Obama had decided to run for the presidency.

PRESIDENTIAL CANDIDATE

Many Democratic candidates vied for the presidential nomination in advance of the 2008 race. Perhaps the most notable was Senator Hillary Clinton from New York, the wife of former U.S. president Bill Clinton. Clinton had not formally announced her decision to seek the presidency, but she had already begun hiring staffers, and rumors suggested that she would be a formidable candidate if she did run. She announced her decision to seek office soon after Obama announced the formation of his exploratory committee.

Although Obama and Clinton emerged as the frontrunners, there were other experienced politicians seeking the Democratic nomination, including former vice-presidential nominee John Edwards (who had also served as senator from North Carolina), Iowa governor Tom Vilsack, Senator Joe Biden of Delaware, Governor Bill Richardson of New Mexico, and Cleveland congressman Dennis Kucinich. There was an equally crowded—and qualified—list of candidates seeking the Republican nomination.

The presence of so many experienced politicians seeking their party's nomination soon gave rise to questions about the strengths and weaknesses of each candidate. Most experts agreed that Obama's greatest weakness was his apparent lack of experience. If he won the nomination, he would have the shortest tenure in statewide office of any nominee from either party since 1952, when first-term Illinois governor Adlai Stevenson challenged Dwight Eisenhower, who had not held elective office. Obama decided to address the question head-on, noting in an interview with CNN, "I think the important thing is not experience per se. Donald Rumsfeld [former Defense Secretary under President George W. Bush] and Dick Cheney [the then-current vice president] had the best resumes in Washington and initiated a fiasco in Iraq."

On February 10, 2007, on a bitterly cold day, Obama stood on the steps of the Old State Capitol in Springfield, Illinois, and formally announced his decision to seek the presidency. In his speech, he acknowledged his lack of national experience in a way that seemed to suggest it could be viewed as an advantage: "I recognize there is a certain presumptuousness—a certain audacity—to this announcement. I know I haven't spent a lot of time learning the ways of Washington. But I've been there long enough to know that the ways of Washington must change."

Race was also an issue in the campaign—not as openly acknowledged, but lurking in the background nonetheless. This was true not only as Obama sought the Democratic nomination but in the broader picture—was America ready for an African-American president? When asked this question by *Newsweek,* Obama's response was firm:

> I absolutely think America is ready. . . . Stereotypes and prejudices still exist in American society, and for the highest office in the land a female or African American candidate would, at the outset, confront some additional hurdles to show that they were qualified and competent. But what I've found is that the American people—once they get to know you—are going to judge you on your individual character.

The numbers were against Obama, however. Only two blacks had been elected state governor since Reconstruction—Douglas Wilder of Virginia and Deval Patrick of Massachusetts—and Obama was the only black senator then serving in the U.S. Senate and one of only three who had ever held a Senate seat.

Building his campaign on hope, on a change from "old-school politics," had certain risks. Prospective voters who responded positively to Obama often did so because they respected his life story and liked his call for a new approach to politics. Precisely what this meant varied from person to person, though. As Obama began to speak more specifically about his positions, some people were surprised to find his positions on issues more liberal than theirs, while others discovered that religion was an important part of his life.

Obama quickly built a substantial campaign fund from donations that totaled some $25 million only two months after he announced his intention to seek the presidency. Concerns about his safety, though, and the large crowds who gathered for his campaign appearances, inspired the Secret Service to place him under their protection early in May 2007.

A CAMPAIGN FOCUSING ON CHANGE

Obama's campaign Web site listed the issues that formed the core of his campaign. Many were the same issues he had championed in the Senate: strengthening America overseas, developing a plan to end the Iraq War, creating a healthcare system that works, developing a national energy policy that moves the United States toward energy independence, improving

Candidate for President

On February 10, 2007, Barack Obama announced that he was seeking the Democratic nomination for president in 2008. He spoke of his background, and the journey that had brought him to Illinois and to this moment. Finally, he invoked the memory of another senator from Illinois who had become president:

By ourselves . . . change will not happen. Divided, we are bound to fail. But the life of a tall, gangly, self-made Springfield lawyer tells us that a different future is possible. He tells us that there is power in words. He tells us that there is power in conviction.

That beneath all the differences of race and region, faith and station, we are one people. He tells us that there is power in hope. As Lincoln organized the forces arrayed against slavery, he was heard to say: "Of strange, discordant, and even hostile elements, we gathered from the four winds, and formed and fought to battle through."

That is our purpose here today. That's why I'm in this race. Not just to hold an office, but to gather with you to transform a nation.

I want to win that next battle—for justice and opportunity. I want to win that next battle—for better schools, and better jobs, and health care for all.

I want us to take up the unfinished business of perfecting our union, and building a better America.

American schools, protecting the American homeland, addressing concerns about immigration and border security, protecting the right to vote, honoring U.S. veterans, cleaning up Washington's "culture of corruption," strengthening families and communities, and reconciling faith and politics.

As Obama emerged as one of the front-runners, scrutiny intensified. In one speech, Obama noted that the 1965 voting rights march in Selma, Alabama, had so inspired his parents that it brought them together and he was the result, stating, "So they got together and Barack Obama Jr. was born." Critics quickly jumped on the statement, noting that Obama was born in 1961, four years before the march took place. Obama later clarified that he had been speaking metaphorically, referencing the civil rights movement as a whole rather than any one event. An ad critical of Hillary Clinton was posted on YouTube and was quickly linked to a political operative working for a firm hired by the Obama campaign, although he stated that he had created the ad independently, not under the direction of Obama or his staffers. Obama's admission of drug use as a young man also caused critics to question his judgment. Still, huge crowds gathered at every Obama rally. Many Democrats began to wonder what an Obama presidency would be like.

In *The Audacity of Hope*, Obama gave a hint about his priorities when describing the things that made him a Democrat:

> This idea that our communal values, our sense of mutual responsibility and social solidarity, should express themselves not just in the church or the mosque or the synagogue; not just on the blocks where we live, in the places where we work, or within our own families; but also through our government. Like many conservatives, I believe in the power of culture to determine both individual success and social cohesion, and I believe we ignore cultural factors at our peril. But I also believe that our government can play a role in shaping that culture for the better—or for the worse.

Above, Democratic presidential hopeful Barack Obama greets supporters as he arrives in Minneapolis, Minnesota, to begin his campaign there.

By January 30, 2008, the Democratic candidates had been trimmed down to just two: senators Barack Obama and Hillary Clinton. Any illusions of a clear front-runner quickly subsided, however, as both senators inspired strong groups of vocal supporters. On February 5, each with two primary wins, Obama and Clinton entered Super Tuesday—the day with the most primaries during the nomination process—hoping to establish a strong lead. The day ended with Obama taking 13 states—4 more than Clinton did—but Clinton stayed in the game by winning the strategically important states of California and New York. Over the next month, Obama won 10 primaries in a row, a devastating blow to the Clinton campaign. Once again all eyes were on the delegate-rich states; this time the battlegrounds were Ohio and Texas. While Clinton won in Ohio, the vote in Texas was split due to the way the delegates were divided.

In the tightest nomination race in recent history, Obama and Clinton continued on with their campaigns. Clinton emphasized her long experience as a senator and first lady. Obama under-scored his early opposition to the Iraq War and his ability to be a fresh, unifying force in Washington. Focusing on the ideas of hope and change, Obama's skill as an orator—the talent that launched his rise to prominence at the 2004 Democratic national convention—inspired extensive grassroots support. Early in the race, Obama set the tone that would dominate much of his campaign. In his speech following his loss of the New Hampshire primary, he declared:

> For when we have faced down impossible odds, when we've been told we're not ready or that we shouldn't try or that we can't, generations of Americans have responded with a simple creed that sums up the spirit of a people: Yes, we can. Yes, we can. Yes, we can.
>
> It was a creed written into the founding documents that declared the destiny of a nation: Yes, we can.
>
> It was whispered by slaves and abolitionists as they blazed a trail towards freedom through the darkest of nights: Yes, we can.
>
> It was sung by immigrants as they struck out from distant shores and pioneers who pushed westward against an unforgiving wilderness: Yes, we can.
>
> It was the call of workers who organized, women who reached for the ballot, a president who chose the moon as our new frontier, and a king who took us to the mountaintop and pointed the way to the promised land: Yes, we can, to justice and equality.
>
> Yes, we can, to opportunity and prosperity. Yes, we can heal this nation. Yes, we can repair this world. Yes, we can….
>
> We will remember that there is something happening in America, that we are not as divided as our politics suggest, that we are one people, we are one nation.
>
> And, together, we will begin the next great chapter in the American story, with three words that will ring from coast to coast, from sea to shining sea: Yes, we can.

Soon after, a popular musician and bevy of celebrity supporters produced a video that transformed Obama's speech into a song, overlaid by vocals and guitar. The "Yes, We Can" video quickly gained more than 20 million viewings through Web sites such as YouTube.com. Such grassroots actions reflected Obama's large number of young supporters. Among youth, African Americans, and southerners, Obama found a strong base of support. Other groups, including labor organizations, also gave their support to Obama, surprising many observers. Yet a tight race between the two strong contenders continued into late spring 2008.

At the conclusion of the last state primaries on June 3, Obama passed the delegate mark to become the presumptive Democratic nominee. On June 7, 2008, Hillary Clinton announced that she was suspending her campaign and endorsing Obama for president.

Obama is the first African-American candidate to lead either the Democrats or Republicans in the presidential race. While issues of race and gender marked the primary campaigns to some degree, for the most part the fight was led by the candidates's platforms: Clinton's experience versus Obama's promise of change.

A CANDIDATE'S LEGACY

The true significance of Barack Obama's quest for the presidency in 2008 was not whether his campaign ended in defeat or in success. It was instead for what Obama represented to millions of Americans, who expressed a desire for change and believed that he represented that change, that different approach to government. They saw in his discussion of "the audacity of hope" a reflection of their own hopes and dreams for themselves, their families, and their country.

To many, Obama's very candidacy—and the overwhelming response to his campaign—was a sign that the civil rights movement had entered a new era. It was an era in which Americans looked to an African American and saw their future, a future of hope and promise.

1961 Barack Obama is born on August 4, in Honolulu, Hawaii.

1963 His father leaves the family to attend Harvard.

1967 Obama moves with his mother to Jakarta, Indonesia.

1971 He goes back to Hawaii to attend Punahou Academy.

1979 He graduates high school and begins studies at Occidental College in California.

1981 He transfers to Columbia University in New York.

1982 Obama's father dies in November.

1983 Obama graduates from Columbia.

1985 He begins work as a community organizer in Chicago.

1988 He travels to Kenya; enrolls in Harvard Law School.

1990 He becomes first black president of *Harvard Law Review*.

1991 He earns law degree from Harvard; returns to Chicago.

1992 He organizes new voter registration drive; marries wife, Michelle.

1995 *Dreams From My Father* is published.

1996 Obama is elected to the Illinois Senate.

2000 He challenges incumbent Bobby Rush for the 1st U.S. Congressional District seat and is defeated.

2003 He begins campaign for the U.S. Senate.

2004 Obama wins senatorial primary on March 16; delivers keynote address at Democratic National Convention in Boston on July 27; is elected senator on November 2.

2006 *The Audacity of Hope* is published.

2007 Announces his decision to become a candidate for president on February 10.

2008 Hillary Clinton suspends her presidential campaign and endorses Obama, the presumptive Democratic nominee, on June 7.

Daley, James, ed. *Great Speeches by African Americans.* New York: Dover Publications, 2006.

Obama, Barack. *The Audacity of Hope.* New York: Crown Publishers, 2006.

———. *Dreams From My Father.* New York: Three Rivers Press, 2004.

Orr, Marion, ed. *Transforming the City: Community Organizing and the Challenge of Political Change.* Lawrence: University Press of Kansas, 2007.

Rogak, Lisa, ed. *Barack Obama: In His Own Words.* New York: Carroll & Graf, 2007.

WEB SITES

Barack Obama: U.S. Senator for Illinois
http://www.obama.senate.gov

Join the Movement: Obama '08
http://www.barackobama.com

"The Living Room Candidate: Presidential Campaign Commercials, 1952–2004," American Museum of the Moving Image
http://livingroomcandidate.movingimage.us

Obama's Keynote Address
http://www.pbs.org/newshour/vote2004/demconvention/speeches/obama.html

"The Presidential Field: Barack Obama," Washingtonpost.com
http://projects.washingtonpost.com/2008-presidential-candidates/barack-obama/

"The U.S. Congress Votes Database," Washingtonpost.com
http://projects.washingtonpost.com/congress/members/o000167/key-votes/

A

Abortion issues, 83
African American
  history, 47
  identity, 33, 35
  in politics, 39, 55–56, 70, 74–75,
    78, 86, 91
  students, 34, 37, 55
Ali, Muhammad, 81
Al Qaeda, 69
Atgeld gardens, 40–43
Audacity of Hope, The
  American values in, 68
  campaigns in, 71–72, 78–79
  as a community organizer in, 38,
    52, 72
  faith in, 48–49
  mother in, 14
  political issues in, 60, 64, 66, 82,
    88–89
  publication, 82–83
  racism in, 14, 53
  as a Senator in, 81
Avian flu, 82

B

Baldwin, James, 33
Barker, Kim
  on Obama, 19, 25, 33
Baron, Michael, 36
Berenson, Bradford, 55
Biden, Joe, 85
Black Panthers, 64–65
Braun, Carol Moseley, 75
Brown v. Board of Education, 3
Bush, George, H.W., 82
Bush, George W., 85
  administration, 55, 67–68, 75

C

Cheney, Dick, 85
Chicago, 55
  community organizer in, 37–49,
    52–53, 56
  ghettos in, 39–42

lawyer in, 33
politics, 59–79
return to, 52, 57–58
Civil Rights, 31
  activists, 23, 37, 65, 88–89
  cases, 57–58
  legislative actions, 63, 83
Civil War, 13
Clinton, Bill, 82, 85
Clinton, Hillary, 85, 88, 89-91
Columbia University, 35–36
Communism, 17
Community organizer
  in Chicago, 37–49, 52–53, 56, 72
  neighborhood cleanups, 41–42
Congo, 82
Crime
  and the death penalty, 60, 62
  issues related to, 60

D

Daley, Richard, 71
Davis, Jefferson, 13
Declaration of Independence, 68
Democratic National Convention
  keynote address at, 4, 75–77, 83, 90
Developing Communities Project
  (DCP)
  work with, 39, 42–43, 46–47
Dillard, Kirk, 62
*Dreams From My Father: A Story of
  Race and Inheritance* (autobiography)
  American law in, 3
  basketball in, 31
  childhood in, 7, 16, 18–20, 27
  community organizer in, 43
  father in, 36–37, 45–46, 50
  drug use in, 33–34
  identity in, 9, 15
  politics in, 59
  publication, 56–57
  racism in, 3–33
Du Bois, W.E.B., 33
Dunham, Madelyn (grandmother),

14, 38, 64
living with, 13, 16–18, 23,
  25–28, 30
Dunham, Stanley (grandfather),
  8, 14, 35
living with, 13, 16–17, 23,
  25–28, 30
military, 4, 13, 76
Dunham, Stanley Ann (mother),
  38
growing up, 4, 7–8, 12–15, 72
occupations, 20, 28, 34
relationships, 4, 15–16, 18,
  21–22, 27, 36
Durbin, Richard, 81

E

Education
  programs for, 60–61, 65, 82, 84
Eisenhower, Dwight, 85
Environmental issues
  air pollution, 67
  alternative energy, 81–82, 84, 87
  wetlands, 67

F

Feingold, Russell, 76
Fitzgerald, Peter, 74

G

Gandhi, Mahatma, 81
Government ethics
  legislation, 64, 82
  priorities, 72, 88
  spending, 81
Great Britain
  African settlements, 10–11
  military, 11
Great Depression, 13
Gun control, 62, 64–65

H

Harvard Law Review
  president, 55–56
  working on, 52

Harvard Law School, 47, 70
  years at, 50, 52–58
Harvard University, 15, 44, 50
Health Care Justice Act, 63
Homeland security, 82
Honolulu, Hawaii
  family in, 64
  growing up in, 7, 15, 18, 23, 25,
    27, 34, 38, 46, 72
Hull, Blair, 72
Hurricane Katrina, 82
Hussein, Saddam, 68
Hynes, Dan, 74

I

Illinois state senator
  campaign for, 46–47, 58–59
  committees, 60
  issues during, 60–64
  years as, 3, 58, 60–64, 67, 72, 82
Immigration issues, 82, 87
Indonesia
  government, 17
  language and culture, 18, 21
  living in, 17–19, 72
  military, 17, 20
  mother in, 28, 34
Iraq war, 4, 90
  protests again, 67–69, 85, 87
  troops in, 82

K

Kakugawa, Keith, 31, 34
Kennedy, John F., 81
Kenya
  family in, 37, 43–45, 50
  father growing up in, 4, 7–8, 15,
    25, 76
  government, 44–45
  independence movement in,
    11–12, 26, 44
  Luo tribe in, 8–9, 23
  roots in, 8–11
  travel to, 8–10, 50–52
Kenyatta, Jomo, 8

Kerry, John, 4, 75
Keyes, Alan, 77–79
King, Martin Luther, Jr., 22–23, 81
Klein, Joe, 62
Kucinich, Dennis, 85
Kusonoki, Eric, 28

L

Lincoln, Abraham, 72, 81, 87
  assassination, 1
  "House Divided" speech, 1–2
Love, Alvin, 43
Lugar, Richard, 82

M

Malcolm X, 33
Mandela, Nelson, 81
Marshall, Thurgood, 81
Military, 4, 7, 31
  veterans issues, 82, 88
  at war, 10, 67–69, 82, 85
Miner, Barnhill & Galland law
  firm, 57
Muslim
  customs, 20
  in Indonesia, 20–21

N

New York City
  living in, 35–36

O

Obama, Akumu Hussein (grandmother), 10–11
Obama, Auma (half-sister), 37
  meeting, 43–46
  visiting, 50
Obama, Barack, Sr. (father)
  abandonment of family, 8,
    15–16
  children and wives, 25, 36, 43,
    45–46, 50
  death, 9–10, 36, 44, 52
  education, 15, 22, 44, 50

growing up, 4, 7, 11–12, 50, 72,
  76
influence of, 15
meeting again, 8, 15, 26, 36,
  45–46
occupations, 44–45
Obama, Barack, Jr.
  and basketball, 29–31
  birth, 7–8
  childhood, 8, 13, 15–27, 38
  chronology, 90–91
  education, 20, 23–28, 33–35
  identity and alienation, 9, 15,
    22–23, 25–26, 33, 35, 38, 52
  marriage, 57
  troubled youth, 27–37, 88
Obama, Hussein Onyango
  (grandfather), 10–11
Obama, Malia (daughter), 64, 67
Obama, Michelle Robinson
  (wife)
  family, 54–55, 64, 80
  marriage, 57
  meeting, 53–54
Obama, Natasha (daughter), 64
Obama, Roy (brother), 44–45
Occidental College, 34–35
Overall, George Washington, 12

P

Parks, Rosa, 22
Patrick, Deval, 86
Patton, George S., 4, 13
Pearl Harbor, 4, 13
"Pop" (poem), 35
Presidential campaign
  announcement to run, 2–4, 6,
    12, 85–87
  exploratory committee, 84–85
  funds, 87
  issues, 3–5, 86–91
  running, 19, 83–91
Punahou School
  basketball team, 30
  years at, 23–25, 27–28

R

Racism, 13–14
  and profiling, 62
  views on, 31–33, 35, 53, 56, 72, 86
Reagan, Ronald, 78
Rezko, Tony, 83–84
Richardson, Bill, 85
Roberts, John, 82–83
Rogers, Steven S., 70
Rumsfeld, Donald, 85
Rush, Bobby, 64–66
Ryan, Jack, 74

S

Santorum, Rick, 82
Scharnberg, Kirsten
  on Obama, 19, 25, 33
Secret Service, 87
Senate, United States
  campaign for, 67, 70–79
  committees and issues, 81–84,
    87
  election, 6, 74–75, 79
  only black member, 74–75, 86
  race for, 67–69
  voting record, 4
  work in, 3, 80–89
Senior citizen support, 82
Soetoro, Lolo (step-father), 16, 27
  influence of, 18–19, 21–22
  military, 17, 20
Soetoro, Maya (half-sister), 21
  childhood, 27–28, 38
  on Obama, 33
South Africa
  government, 35
Southern New Hampshire University
  commencement speech at,
    48–49
Soviet Union, 82
Speeches
  "Audacity of Hope," 4–6, 75–77,
    83
  commencement at Southern

New Hampshire University,
  48–49
presidential announcement,
  2–4, 6, 85–86
Spiva, Bruce, 55
Springfield, Illinois
  the capitol in, 1–2, 4, 6, 85–86
  political career in, 3, 58
Stevenson, Adlai, 85
Suharto, General, 17
Supreme Court, 83
Syverson, Dave, 62

T

Taxes and budgets
  programs, 60, 62, 64, 81
Town hall meetings, 81
Trinity United Church of Christ,
  47–49

U

United States Congress
  changes in, 3–4
  Senators, 1
  unsuccessful run for, 64–66,
    70–71
Universal health care
  ways to implement, 3, 63, 65, 82,
    84, 87
University of Chicago, 70
  teaching at, 58
University of Hawaii
  basketball team, 29–30
  parents at, 8, 15–16, 44

V

Video game effects, 82
Vilsack, Tom, 85

W

Wallace-Wells, Benn, 72, 80
Washington, Harold, 39
World War II, 10, 76
Wright, Jeremiah, 47
  influence of, 48–49

About the Author

Heather Lehr Wagner is the author of more than 30 books exploring social and political issues and focusing on the lives of prominent men and women. She earned a B.A. in political science from Duke University and an M.A. in government from the College of William and Mary. She lives with her husband and family in Pennsylvania.

Picture Credits

PAGE

2: AP Images, Charles Rex Arbogast
5: AP Images, Stephan Savoia
9: © Jacob Wire/epa/Corbis
19: © Sergio Dorantes/Corbis
24: Courtesy of Punahou School
29: Courtesy of Punahou School
32: Courtesy of Punahou School
41: AP Images, Charles Rex Arbogast
51: Courtesy Harvard News Office

54: AP Images, Jae C. Hong
57: Courtesy Harvard News Office
61: AP Images, Seth Perlman
63: AP Images, M. Spencer Green
66: AP Images, Yuri Gripas
73: AP Images, Seth Perlman
78: AP Images, Nam Y Huh
84: AP Images, Richard Carson
89: AP Images, Jim Mone